Black Bean Soup	65
Roasted Butternut Squash Soup	66
Roasted Tomato Soup	66
Cauliflower & Smoked Gouda Soup	67
Creamy Asparagus Potato Soup	67
Creamy Broccoli Soup	68
Winter Minestrone	69
Hungarian Beef Stew	70
White Turkey Chili	70
Amber Ale Turkey Chili	71
Spicy Chicken Chili	72
Vegan Black Bean Espresso Chili	72
Paleo Chili	73

Main Meals

No-Fail Roasted Chicken Breasts	76
Whole Roasted Chicken	76
Feta, Herb & Sundried Tomato Stuffed Chicken	77
Chicken Thighs with Chimichurri Sauce	78
Farrotto with Mushrooms & Vegetables	78
Quinoa Risotto with Lemon & Roasted Tomatoes	79
Shrimp & Tomato Risotto	80
Spanish-Style Quinoa with Chicken or Steak	80
Sweet Potato & Chicken Fajitas	81
Chili-Rubbed Steak Tacos	81
Turkey Taco Lettuce Cups	82
Herbed Turkey Burgers	82
Veggie Burgers	83
Lemon-Roasted Salmon	84
Pistachio & Broccoli-Crusted Salmon	84
Citrusy Salmon with Kale & Barley	85
Couscous with Shrimp & Green Beans	85
Garlicky Prawns	86
Chermoula Fish Fillets	86
Halibut with Lentils & Mustard Sauce	87
Fennel-Crusted Pork Loin with Potatoes, Onions & Pears	87
Herb-Crusted Pork Loin	88
Beef Tagine with Butternut Squash	88
Sirloin Steak with Garlic Butter	89
Pepper-Crusted Beef Tenderloin	89
Coconut Ginger Chicken with Rice & Vegetables	90
Green Chicken Curry	91
Indian Dal	91
Teriyaki Salmon Stir Fry	92
Chicken & Broccoli Stir Fry	93

Dessert

Spiced Peach & Pistachio Crisp	96
Apple & Pear Crisp	96
Baked Fruit Crumble	97
Pear, Fig & Pecan Galette	97
Summer Peach/Plum Galette	98
Chocolate Mousse	99
Honey Vanilla Chia Pudding	99
Coconut Banana Pudding	100
Chocolate Stout Brownies	100
Chocolate Zucchini Bread	101
Pumpkin Chocolate Chip Bread	101
Blueberry Oat Bars	102
Zucchini Banana Bars	102
Grilled Nectarines with Balsamic Vinegar	103

Condiments & Dressings

Guilt-Free Guacamole	106
Traditional Guacamole	106
Pico de Gallo	106
Mango Salsa	106
Avocado Lime Salsa	107
Spicy Peach Salsa	107
Avocado Hummus	108
White Bean Dip	108
Simple Vinaigrette Dressing	109
Cilantro Lime Dressing	109
Orange Herb Dressing	109
Balsamic Dressing	109
Smoky Barbecue Dressing	110
Red Wine Vinaigrette Dressing	110
Savory Tahini Dressing	110

Other Recipes

Almond Milk	114
Chicken Stock	114
Honey Vanilla Granola	115
Parmesan Kale Chips	115
Herbed Cashew Cheese	116
Kale Pesto	117
Basil Pesto	117
Avocado Spinach Pesto	117
Chimichurri Sauce	117
Gluten-free Flour Blend	119

About the Author   120

Why Cook at Home?

Why do I want to inspire you to cook at home more often? There are so many reasons, including potentially helping you live longer. It's also one of the best strategies for healthy eating since you control the ingredients, the preparation and the portions you serve. Of course cooking takes more time than picking up takeout or pre-prepared foods. But the time you invest in preparing your own meals is more than worth it because ...

You save money. Prepared or restaurant-cooked food is always going to be more expensive than the whole ingredients. You pay for the convenience of someone else doing the work—often more than you think! Restaurants typically mark up all food about three times what it cost them to buy the ingredients they use. Plus, you have no control over the quality of those ingredients. Those takeout dishes could contain additives, extra sugar and salt or fats, or even genetically modified ingredients (GMOs).

You keep your stomach happy. It's not rare anymore to hear stories about food safety violations or contamination. In any given week, you can usually find an article or two about a recall, a restaurant being shut down or cited for health code violations, or people getting sick from food they ate out. By cooking at home, you control food handling, prep and the cleanliness of your tools and kitchen, so food-borne illness or contamination becomes much less of an issue.

You gain more quality time with family and friends. Sitting down for meals together as often as possible can make it a lot easier to maintain a sense of connection with your immediate family. Eating together helps kids and teens alike learn manners, develop a strong sense of belonging, and it gives parents a chance to give their children dedicated time and attention. Get your kids cooking with you and they will be more likely to eat a wider variety of foods. Plus, you'll be teaching them healthy eating habits they'll have for the rest of their lives. Preparing and sharing home-cooked meals with friends provides an opportunity to connect over something positive and healthy and teach each other new recipes.

You can be more self-reliant. What if you were stranded in the woods for a couple days? What would happen if you couldn't get to the store or get takeout? The first scenario probably won't happen. The second absolutely will at some point. But, if you have no idea how to cook, it leaves you pretty helpless, right? Learning basic skills and then branching out as you grow in experience and confidence will leave you less dependent on others—family, friends, the food industry, the grocery store or restaurants—to feed you.

These all sound great, right? So, why don't more of us cook? Usually, it's because we think we ...

- Don't have the time (this is the #1 reason people cite)
- Don't have the equipment
- Don't have the skill
- Don't know what to make
- Don't know how to plan and prep (which can really reduce the work involved)

I want to help you feel confident in the kitchen so you feel comfortable preparing more of your own meals at home. This recipe guide will help you understand the basics, provide you with a wide variety of options so you don't get bored and help make cooking more efficient and fun.

> One Public Health Nutrition study found that people who cook at least five times a week are 47 percent more likely to be alive 10 years later compared to those who rely more on processed foods.

I created this book because as a personal trainer, my clients were constantly asking me what I ate to lose fat or maintain fat loss. So, I started sharing some of the recipes I use and the tips and tricks I'd learned preparing more of my own meals, and I could quickly see the difference it made in their efforts toward better health and fitness. By choosing more whole foods and preparing more of their own meals, my clients had more energy, lost more excess body fat, and looked and felt better.

My goal for this recipe book is simple. I want to inspire you to cook. Why? Because the basic truth is, the more you cook, the better you look. Let's get one thing clear from the start though—this is not about going on a diet. There are no "diet" foods here. Who wants to eat food that tastes like cardboard? Who wants to feel deprived? I certainly don't! I know from years of experience that the best success comes from not depriving yourself of wonderful food, but from learning how to prepare delicious foods that nourish your body and that you enjoy eating.

I could rhapsodize all day about great food and cheerfully spend hours browsing in farmer's markets, at kitchen stores and talking with other foodies about great food. However, I know that not everyone shares this passion or has the time or energy to make elaborate meals. You may have more time to dedicate in the kitchen. Or you may not. Either way, this book will give you some clever ways to make your time in the kitchen both more enjoyable and less time consuming.

In these pages you will find more than 100 delicious, easy to make recipes I've created or curated and tweaked to make healthier. I hope you enjoy my notes and insights about the recipes as well.

Ready to get cooking?

In health,

Contents

Why Cook at Home?	6
Basic Cooking Terms	7
The Right Tools for the Job	8
Cooking with Oils	10
Planning & Prep Tips	12
Shopping for Ingredients	14
Produce Tips	16
Meat & Poultry Tips	18
Fish & Seafood Tips	19
Grocery Shopping Tips	19

Recipe Key
Watch for the symbols d g underneath the recipe title. Those indicate whether that recipe is dairy-free and/or gluten-free.

Breakfast

Kale, Sausage & Leek Frittata	22
Feta, Asparagus & Green Onion Frittata	24
Asparagus & Mushroom Scramble	24
Spinach Avocado Pesto Scramble	25
Breakfast Bowl	25
Avocado Breakfast Bake	26
Roasted Asparagus & Arugula Breakfast Salad	26
Potato, Kale & Sausage Breakfast Hash	27
Chicken & Sweet Potato Breakfast Hash	28
Smoked Salmon Avocado Toast	28
Basic Protein Pancakes	29
Blood Orange Zucchini Pancakes	30
Buckwheat Banana Pancakes	31
Coconut Berry Oatmeal Bake	31
Warm & Nutty Quinoa	32
Savory Oatmeal	32

Smoothies

Lemony Green Smoothie	36
Blueberry Kale Smoothie	36
Greens & Beans Smoothie	36
Vanilla Latte Energizer Smoothie	37
Almond Butter Smoothie	37
Banana Blackberry Smoothie	37

Sides

Balsamic & Parmesan Cauliflower	40
Cauliflower Rice (three ways)	41
Garlic & Sage Spaghetti Squash	42
Mashed Squash with Caramelized Onions	42
Honey-Roasted Butternut Squash	43
Rosemary Roasted Beets & Carrots	43
Brussels Sprouts with Pancetta & Sage	44
Farro with Wild Mushrooms & Herbs	44
Risotto-Style Barley with Asparagus	45
Roasted Sweet Potatoes/Fries	45
Balsamic Roasted Vegetables	46
Roasted Fennel with Pears, Parmesan & Thyme	46
Asparagus with Orange Honey Glaze	47
Asparagus with Lemon & Pecorino	47
Parmesan Rosemary Polenta	48
Savory Black Beans	48
Green Bean & Garlic Sauté	49
Broccolini Sauté	49
Roasted Broccolini with Winey Mushrooms	49

Salads

Heirloom Tomato Salad	52
Lentil Salad	53
Sicilian Farro & Tuna Salad	53
Mexican Quinoa Salad	54
Simple Avocado Quinoa Salad	54
Israeli Salad	55
Greek Vegetable Salad	55
Summer Panzanella Salad	56
Kale & Stonefruit Salad	56
Kale, Grains & Blueberry Salad	57
Kale, Avocado & Carrot Salad	57
Apple, Carrot & Cabbage Chop	58
Southwestern Chopped Salad	58
Roasted Vegetable & Farro Salad	59
Arugula & Radicchio Pizza Salad	59

Soups, Stews & Chili

Chicken Tortilla Soup	62
Classic Chicken & Vegetable Soup	63
Chicken & Wild Rice Soup	63
White Bean & Kale Soup	64
Spicy Shrimp, Farro & Greens Soup	64

Basic Cooking Terms

What's the difference between baking and broiling? Chopping and dicing? Sautéing and dry-sautéing? There are lots of cooking terms that commonly appear in recipes. Here are some of the basic ones you should know.

Au jus. Serving meat in its own natural sauces from cooking without adding anything to it.

Blanch and shock. Boiling briefly in water (blanch) and then cooling quickly with an ice bath (shock). This technique is the best way to preserve color and nutrients in vegetables and helps firm the flesh of a fruit while loosening the skins, making peeling easier.

Boil. Cooking in a rapidly bubbling liquid.

Braise. Cooking covered in a small amount of liquid after a preliminary browning or searing. An excellent method for tougher cuts of meat.

Broil. Cooking with radiant heat from above. Sometimes used to finish a dish for a few minutes at the end of cooking.

Chop. Cutting into irregularly-shaped pieces.

Crush. Using the side of your knife to press or smash. Garlic cloves are often prepped this way.

Dice. Cutting into even, small, square-shaped pieces.

Dry-sauté. Cooking food in a hot pan with nothing in it (no oil, butter, water, spaces). Do this over medium-high heat and stir often to prevent burning. The heat will release the liquids in food and give them a nice texture.

Emulsify. Combining two liquids that normally don't mix (like oil and vinegar) into a creamy, unified concoction. Dispersing and suspending tiny droplets of one liquid throughout the other takes some patience, so don't rush the process.

Grill. Cooking directly over a heat source, such as an outdoor barbecue. Not just for meats, grilling is a great option for veggies and summer fruits, too.

Julienne. Cutting into short, thin strips.

Mince. Cutting into very small pieces.

Mise en place. A French term that means having all of your ingredients prepared and ready to go before you start cooking so you can focus only on cooking rather than prepping and cooking.

Pan-fry. Cooking in a moderate amount of fat over medium heat. Skin-on salmon with salt and pepper or salt-free blackening spice is amazing prepared this way.

Poach. Cooking in a small amount of hot liquid kept at a low simmer (just a few bubbles around the pan). Poaching allows for more wiggle room to cook a recipe just right, making it a go-to for a plump chicken breast or fillets of fish that can easily overcook or cook unevenly at high heat.

Roast or bake. Cooking by surrounding food with hot air, as in the oven. "Roast" often applies to meats and poultry but can refer to veggies, while "bake" can also apply to veggies, fish, poultry and baked goods of course!

Sauté. Cooking quickly in a small amount of fat like olive oil, coconut oil or butter.

Sear. Creating a crisp, golden brown exterior on meat or fish. Transfer thicker cuts, like steak or pork tenderloin to the oven to cook to a rosy medium rare.

Simmer. Cooking in a gently simmering liquid.

Slow roast. Cooking "low and slow" helps get the most flavor out of vegetables and ensures an even, fork-tender finish on a large cut of meat. High heat can dry out the edges before the center is cooked.

Steam. Cooking foods by exposing them to direct steam, such as in your large pot with the steamer basket (colander) that fits inside.

Reduce. Simmering or boiling liquid until the volume decreases. Often used to render a more concentrated, thicker product. An invaluable technique for simple sauces.

Rest. Removing from heat and tenting with foil or just letting sit prior to cutting and serving. This is a critical step when cooking meat, poultry and fish to let the juices settle and keep the protein moist and juicy!

Right Tools for the Job

Cooking at home starts with having the right tools for the job. By now, you probably have many of the basics in your kitchen, like:

- Spoons, ladles, spatulas, whisks and metal tongs
- Measuring spoons and cups
- Knives and kitchen shears
- Mixing bowls in a variety of sizes
- Pie, bread and cake pans, muffin tins and glass or ceramic baking dishes
- Storage containers of various sizes (if you are still using plastic or Tupperware, I recommend upgrading to glass ones so you can avoid the chemicals)
- A basic set of pots and pans such as a small and medium-sized sauce pan with lid, an omelet pan or skillet, and flat grilling pan that you use for pancakes are probably ones you already have
- Textured grill pan (the one that makes those nice lines)
- Cutting boards (one for fruits and veggies and one for meats that can be placed in the dish washer for sanitizing)
- Metal box grater
- Fruit and veggie peeler
- Zester

I highly recommend these additional tools to complete outfitting your kitchen. If you choose to invest in these, you can find well-priced options at Bed, Bath & Beyond, Target or online.

1. **Santoku knife.** Typically ranges in size from five to seven inches, but comes in smaller sizes too. They are uniquely styled like a narrow-bladed cleaver, with sharp edges and dimples on the blade that helps to release thin slices and sticky food after slicing.

2. **Serrated chopping knife.** Smaller serrated knives make chopping things like nuts a lot easier since the knife won't slip on the nuts. Look for a four- to five-inch blade.

3. **Sauté pan with lid.** For searing and sautéing meats, vegetables, and chicken. Look for a larger size and choose stainless steel, cast iron or annodized aluminum if possible.

4. **Stir-fry pan.** Great for sautéing vegetables and making stir-fry dishes. They start at about $30 and go up from there. Start with an inexpensive one until you decide that it's worth investing in a nicer one.

5. **Instant-read thermometer.** Allows you to check the cooking temperature of meat, pork and poultry so you know when it's fully cooked. There are many different shapes of these, so buy the one you prefer.

6. **Stockpot with lid.** Something in mid-weight anodized aluminum or stainless steel is a good choice, since you may also want to use your stockpot to make large quantities of soup, stock, or stews. The handles on a stockpot should be big enough to grasp firmly. Some models may come with a removable colander.

7. **Baking sheets.** Baking sheets come in a couple of different formats--rimless and rimmed. Rimless works best for cookies, crusts or things that you may want to slide off easily without breaking. Rimmed works best when you need a lip, or you're working with things that might spill over like homemade granola or toasted nuts.

8. **Nutri-Bullet.** This is the ultimate smoothie and protein shake machine. It can also blend small batches of other things like batter for Protein Pancakes in a pinch. I use mine (the Rx model) to make my own almond milk, too!

9. **Slow cooker.** Inexpensive to buy and easy to use, slow cookers can turn inexpensive cuts of meat or low cost vegetarian dishes into delicious meals with minimal work while you do other things.

10. **Immersion blender.** Also called a stick blender, this gadget is one of the best investments I ever made. Use it to pureé soups into a creamy texture without transferring hot soup to a blender and burning yourself in the process.

11. **Food processor.** A mini one is great for salsas, dips, marinades and dressing. If you'll be making big batches of things like Protein Pancakes or you want to grate veggies or cheese, the larger size is worth the investment. Attachments will let you double it as a mixer for baking or other cooking needs.

12. **Stand mixer.** This wonderful gadget comes with attachments for grinding meat, mixing bread and making your own pasta, in addition to mixing batter or heavy cream. You don't have to make this investment because your food processor can double as a mixer in most cases. But if you've got the money to spend and like shiny kitchen gadgets, this is a useful tool.

> It's important to keep your tools in good condition. Here are a few of my favorite tips to care for yours:
>
> - Be sure to wash your kitchen knives and shears by hand, rather than the dishwasher, which will rust them.
> - Clean cutting boards well with hot, soapy water after each use.
> - Don't put wooden cutting boards in the dishwasher as they will be more likely to crack and dry out.
> - Don't use metal spatulas or utensils on non-stick pans. They will scrape the coating off.

10

7

8

9

12

Cooking with Oils

There are a lot of choices when it comes to oils for cooking. Which ones are the best? It depends on what tastes good to you, the smoke point of the oil and the level of omega-6 fatty acids in the oil. Before you choose oils, learn a little more about the lingo and your options by smoke point.

Label Lingo

Cold-pressed or expeller pressed. The oil is extracted by a machine that presses and grinds the seeds or olives at a low temperature, which helps retain more flavor. No chemicals are used.

Extra-virgin. This is the highest quality and most expensive olive oil classification. It should have no defects and a flavor of fresh olives. It must be produced entirely by mechanical means without the use of any solvents, and under temperatures that will not degrade the oil.

Virgin. It can be heated and used for cooking.

Light. Refers to the flavor of the oil, not the calorie count or fat content.

Pure. It has the highest smoke point and can be used for frying or roasting.

Refined. After extraction, the oil is processed to remove impurities, including pesticides, and bleached. This increases the shelf life and improves the taste and color.

Unrefined. No further processing is done after extraction. These oils can't be used in high-heat cooking, like frying, and they may spoil more quickly than refined varieties. Because pesticides aren't removed, always choose organic when buying unrefined oils.

> When cooking with oils, watch the quantity you use. People often use too much oil and the calories can really add up.
>
> Try to stick to about 2 tablespoons a day—the amount recommended for most adults.

Smoke point is the temperature at which the oil starts to smoke. When an oil reaches its smoke point, it breaks down and harmful substances are created, which means the beneficial compounds of the oil are destroyed. Oils can have low, medium or high smoke points. the oils are listed below are in order from best choice to least favorite choice based on nutritional value/content.

LOW

Oils with low smoke points can't handle heat, so they're best reserved for dressings, marinades and dips.

Extra-virgin olive oil: processed rapidly after the olives are picked and very flavorful; great as a finishing oil, dip or used in dressings. Look for cold-pressed, higher-quality oil.

Walnut oil: heart-healthy, full-flavored and delicious drizzled over veggies or used to dress salads.

Flaxseed oil: like walnut oil, ideal to use in salad dressings or mixed into a smoothie; a great source of omega-3s. Look for cold-pressed, higher-quality oil.

MEDIUM

Oils with medium smoke points are ideal for every day stove-top cooking, sauce-making, stir-frying and oven baking.

Canola oil: Versatile and a great source of monounsaturated fats; has a light flavor that works well in baking and can also be used to coat a barbeque or propane grill.

Coconut oil: Gives foods a delicious light coconut flavor; works well for curries and sautéing tofu, baking and adding a little extra moisture to lips, skin and hair. Look for organic, virgin coconut oil if available.

Olive oil: Perfect for cooking proteins and veggies or making soups and chilis; also good for baking but I prefer to use coconut oil.

Grape-seed oil: Extracted from grape seeds during wine making; earthy flavor and great for sautéing.

Sesame oil: Delicious nutty flavor that adds a nice depth to Asian-inspired dishes.

HIGH

Oils with high smoke points can withstand very high temps, so you can turn up the fire or heat.

Avocado oil: A great source of oleic acid (an essential fatty acid) and vitamin E. It has a very mild to non-existent flavor, so it won't add something unwanted to foods. It's also got some other benefits such as reducing inflammation, strengthening skin and helping your hair grow.

Peanut oil: Monounsaturated, contains essential fatty acids and really lends a peanut flavor to food; another top choice for frying, sautéing or roasting. With most other oils, high temps cause them to change their molecular structure and oxidize, but this doesn't happen with peanut oil. The fats aren't fragile, so they don't get damaged at high heat. It's typically on the inexpensive side compared to olive oil or coconut oil.

Safflower oil: A good source of vitamin E with a mild flavor; can be used in everything from curries to baking.

Sunflower oil. Full of vitamins A, D and E; a good choice for frying.

Planning & Prep Tips

One lesson I teach my clients when it comes to eating healthier foods more consistently is to adopt some simple strategies that will make things easier, require less effort and set themselves up for success.

These are a few of my favorites to get you started. Over time, you'll figure out even more strategies that work best for you.

Three Planning Tips

1. **Read online menus before going out to eat.** Before going out to a restaurant, take a couple of minutes to look at the menu online to see what healthy options might be available and review the descriptions of entreés to understand how dishes are prepared. Knowing what you will likely order before you even sit down will help you stick to that healthy choice. Sometimes, I discover that there really isn't any good option at a particular restaurant, so I'll choose a different restaurant.

2. **Write down what you plan to eat during the week.** I use a weekly meal planner template to write down what I'll be eating at home and account for meals I'll be eating out. The benefit is two-fold: it helps me know what I'll need to make the foods I want to eat all week, and it helps me stick to healthier choices. It also saves me from the "what is there to eat" conversation in my head that happens when I don't plan ahead. I sit staring at the fridge, freezer and pantry, and if I don't have healthy stuff on hand, I end up opting for not so healthy stuff that's quick.

   I created a simple template for my clients to use in planning their meals for the week. You can grab a copy at www.evolvefitnessandcoaching.com/fandh-resources.

3. **Plan for meals and snacks you'll need if you're away from home or from your desk.** This could include bringing your lunch to work. If you're going to be out running errands or be otherwise busy, having snacks with you in the car is a life saver. This strategy has saved my bacon many times when I needed something to eat and there weren't many (or any) healthy options available to me.

Three Preparation Tips

1. **Keep your kitchen stocked with the basics.** Depending on the foods you tend to prepare most often, be sure that you have the basic ingredients on hand at all times to prepare those or other simple dishes. This could include your favorite lean proteins, a variety of fruits, veggies and greens, cooking fats, spices and herbs, and other pantry staples like balsamic vinegar, flour, baking powder and soda, and honey.

2. **Prepare food in advance.** My usual habit is to grill a couple of chicken breasts so I can use them in different meals, like salads, spaghetti squash pasta, etc. I also make large batches of soups, stews and/or chili that I can portion out into separate servings and freeze for use later. Nothing like being able to grab a bowl of chili right out of the freezer and have it ready to go. I also make big batches the Basic Protein or Blood Orange Zucchini Pancakes because they freeze so well. My total prep time is only about an hour to 90 minutes on Saturday or Sunday. Then I'm set for the whole week.

3. **Have portions of healthy snacks ready to grab and go.** Put almonds or a mix of your favorite nuts or something like turkey or buffalo jerky into snack-sized plastic bags you can grab on your way out the door. You could also have a stash of snack bars like Kind, Quest or Bulletproof Protein Bars on hand to slip in your bag. Or you could quickly cut up an apple or grab some baby carrots and celery and put that in your bag for later. None of these things needs to be refrigerated, so they are very portable and will last a while in the car or in your bag. If you like items that need refrigeration like Greek yogurt or a string cheese or a smoothie, consider investing in a mini mini-cooler.

Three Routine Tips

1. **Pick a regular day (or two) for grocery shopping.** I typically book Sundays to grocery shop after I've hiked and enjoyed a healthy breakfast out with friends. That way, I'm shopping after I've exercised (so I'm feeling good and healthy) and I've eaten (so I'm not hungry when shopping, which studies show isn't a good idea). I also shop on Wednesdays if I find I need to pick up some things for meals I want to make later in the week.

2. **Book a regular time every week for food prep.** It doesn't have to be a large amount of time. Like I said, I typically invest about 60 to 90 minutes up front so I don't have to spend so much time assembling meals during the week. That way, it takes me 10 minutes to throw together a nice salad and the grilled chicken breast, or to heat up and serve a bowl of chili with a side salad or veggies. This strategy can benefit you whether you're single or you have a family!

3. **Write down your "go to" options for breakfast, lunch, dinner and snacks.** Put your tendency to be a creature of habit to work for you. Build a "go to meals" list of the things you tend to eat most often. You already know you like them. And having these foods already prepped or the ingredients on hand can lessen those "I don't know what I want to eat" moments. Be sure to revisit this list every month or two and change it up. That will keep you out of a food rut and make sure you're getting the variety of foods you need to cover your nutritional bases.

Just like the Weekly Meal Planner, I created a simple template for my clients. Grab a copy at *www.evolvefitnessandcoaching.com/fandh-resources*.

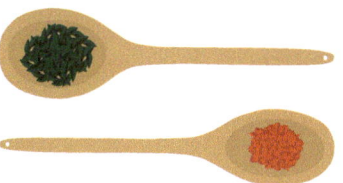

Shopping for Ingredients

There are two truths about food you should understand:

1. **Food is one of the biggest influencers of your hormones.** And since fat loss is primarily about hormones, the food (type, quality, quantity, timing and combination) we eat is a big deal.

2. **We are what we eat (and what we eat, ate).** The source and quality of our food matters because when we ingest foods like animal protein, we are ingesting what that animal ate, what was stored in its fat tissue and how it was treated while alive. Not to mention any antibiotics that it may have been given.

Knowing those two truths, be sure to choose organic, pasture-raised, grass-fed or wild caught animal products that don't use hormones or antibiotics and weren't conventionally raised and choose more nutrient-dense, whole foods over nutritionally deficient, calorically dense processed and fast foods. This section provides some helpful tips on choosing high-quality foods and saving a little money while you're at it.

When to Buy Organic

It's a good idea to buy organic when you can, but you don't have to go organic on everything. When it comes to fruits and veggies, the Environmental Working Group (EWG) maintains two lists of produce known as the Dirty Dozen and the Clean Fifteen that you'll want to become familiar with. Visit EWG's website (*www.ewg.com*) for more information on a variety of products.

- **Burnt orange items are on the Dirty Dozen list.** Dirty Dozen contenders are considered to be the most covered in pesticides. So, invest your food money on going organic on these. Pesticides are endocrine disruptors that can throw off your hormone levels and even lead to weight gain.

- **Green items are on the Clean Fifteen list.** You don't need to spend extra for organic versions unless you want to.

When it comes to animal products, choose the highest quality you can afford. Look for organic, grass-fed, pasture-raised and wild-caught.

> Pesticides are not just insect killers, they're also endocrine disruptors. Because the endocrine system controls metabolism, exposure to certain chemicals can increase appetite, stimulate fat cells, and cause a sluggish metabolism. Pesticide residue on produce like the veggies listed to the right (as well as any plastic packaging they come in) can throw off your hormone levels and even lead to weight gain. Keep eating those fruits and veggies, but be diligent about washing everything, even "pre-washed" salad mixes and foods you won't eat the rind of, such as cantaloupes and avocados. Try submerging them in a large bowl of water for one to two minutes, then rinsing under running water. Use a soft brush to scrub citrus and other foods with hard peels.

Non-starchy Vegetables & Salad Greens (fresh, canned or frozen) * indicate starchy vegetables	Arrowroot*, artichokes, arugula, asparagus (all colors), bamboo shoots, bean sprouts, beans (green, yellow, french), beets, bok choy, broccoli florets, broccolini, broccoli rabe, brussels sprouts, cabbage (all types), carrots*, cauliflower (all colors), celery, chicory, collard greens, cucumbers, eggplant, endive, fennel, green chiles, green onions, hearts of palm, jicama, kale, kohlrabi, leeks, lettuce (any kind except iceberg), mixed greens, mushrooms (all types), mustard greens, okra, olives (any type), onions (red, yellow), parsnips*, peas* (snap, snow), peppers (bell, pepperocini), potato* (red, purple preferably), pumpkin* (fresh or canned), radishes, rutabaga, rhubarb, seaweed, shallots, spinach, spirulina, sprouts, sweet potatoes/yams*, sweet corn*, swiss chard, tomatoes (all varieties), turnips, watercress, zucchini and winter or yellow summer squash*
Fruits (fresh or frozen) * indicate starchy fruits	Apples*, apricots, asian pears, avocados, bananas*, berries (blackberries, boysenberries, raspberries, blueberries, mulberries, strawberries), cantaloupe, cherries, currants (black, dried), dates (fresh or dried), figs (fresh or dried), grapes* (red, green or black), grapefruit, guava, honeydew melon, kiwis, kumquats, lemons, limes, loganberries, mangos, oranges*, nectarines*, papaya, peaches*, pears*, pineapple*, pluots*, plums*, pomegranate (seeds), prunes, tangerines, watermelon Dried fruit such as raisins, currants, blueberries, figs, dates, cherries*
Meat, Poultry, Fish, Seafood & Eggs	Beef (all lean cuts, pasture-raised), buffalo meat (ground), calamari, chicken (skinless, boneless white meat, pasture-raised), clams, cod/scrod fillet, corned beef, crab (lump meat), dory fish fillet, eggs (white, brown, organic omega-3), flounder fillet, game (partridge, pheasant, venison, ostrich, elk), guinea fowl, haddock fillet, halibut fillet, herring, jerky (nitrate-free), lamb (lean cuts), liver, lobster, oysters (packed in water, pancetta, pollock fillet, pork (bacon, chops, tenderloin, loin roast, as high-quality as you can find), rabbit, salmon (wild-caught fillet, nitrate-free smoked), sardines (packed in water), sausage (nitrate-free), scallops, sea bass fillet, shrimp, sole fillet, trout, tuna (solid, white packed in water), turkey (breast meat, lean ground, pasture-raised), turkey bacon (nitrate free)
Legumes (lentils & beans) * all are considered starchy	Black beans, black-eyed peas, edamame (organic, non-GMO), garbanzo beans (chickpeas), kidney beans, lentils (all colors), lima beans, navy beans, pinto beans, split peas
Broth, Herbs, Spices & Condiments	Low-sugar barbeque sauce, brewer's yeast or quick yeast (without gluten), broths (chicken, beef, vegetable; low-sodium, organic), dried herbs (all types), fresh herbs (all types), garlic (fresh, powdered), ginger (fresh), horseradish, braggs liquid aminos, coconut amino acids, tamari, pickles (no sugar added), salsa, seasonings (black and white pepper, chili powder, cinnamon, crushed red pepper, cumin, curry powder, nutmeg, onion salt, raw cacao powder, sea salt), tomato paste, real vanilla extract, vinegar (any type)
Whole Grains & Pods * all are considered starchy	Amaranth, arrowroot, barley, black rice, brown rice (rice, cereal, crackers, flour, pasta, tortillas), buckwheat (groats, flour, pancake mix), farro, kamut (cakes or bread), millet, oats (steel cut or thick rolled), quinoa, spelt (bread, tortillas), wild rice
Nuts, Seeds & Oils	Avocado oil, almonds (raw or dry-roasted without salt), brazil nuts, cashews (raw), chia seeds, coconut oil, flax seeds (ground), hazelnuts (whole) hemp seeds, macadamia nuts (raw), nut butters (almond, cashew, hazelnut, walnut), olive oil (extra-virgin or cold-pressed), pecans, pumpkin seeds, sesame seeds, sunflower seeds, walnuts
Beverages	Any time: Water, green tea, black tea, sparkling water, iced tea, coffee Limited: Red or white wine, hard alcohol (no mixers) such as vodka or whiskey
Dairy & Dairy Alternatives	Almond milk (unsweetened), almond cheese, cashew milk (unsweetened), cashew cheese, coconut milk (unsweetened), coconut milk ice cream, coconut milk yogurt (store-bought or homemade), ghee, hazelnut milk (unsweetened), rice milk (unsweetened), rice cheese, sorbets (fruit or chocolate), soymilk (organic, unsweetened), unsalted grass-fed butter + Try to avoid carrageenan on the ingredients list. It's made of seaweed and used as an emulsifier
Pantry Items	Plant-based protein powders (Arbonne, OptiCleanse, Jay Robb Egg White Protein Powder), collagen protein powder (Upgraded Self), protein bars (Upgraded Self), alternative flours (coconut, tapioca, brown rice, sweet rice, sorghum, buckwheat, gluten-free all purpose), high-quality dark chocolate (70% or higher cacao powder), dark chocolate chips, lentil chips, black bean chips, Mary's Gone Crackers (all flavors), raw organic honey, guacamole, mild salsa, crushed tomatoes, diced tomatoes, unsweetened applesauce, coconut nectar, coconut sugar, Stevia, baking powder, baking soda, brown sugar (for baking), coconut flakes (unsweetened), golden flax meal (for baking), real vanilla extract, all-purpose whole wheat baking flour, xanthan gum (if you will try gluten-free baking), tomato paste, water-packed canned tuna, water-packed salmon

Get a printable version of this list in the free downloads at: **www.evolvefitnessandcoaching.com/fandh-resources**.

Produce Tips

Vegetables, greens and fruit should make up a large part of what you eat. Here are a few helpful tips about buying quality produce and how to store it.

Fresh, Frozen or Canned?

Your best bet for quality produce is to buy fresh, local and in-season whenever you can. At the grocery store, fresh in-season is best, or look for quality frozen options and canned options that don't use extra salt or other ingredients.

Fresh, local produce gets you the most nutrients from your food, particularly if you're getting them from a farmer's market, farmer's produce stand or your own backyard. Plus, if you buy locally, that means less carbon emission and food that retains maximum nutrients.

If you're buying from a grocery store you may not be getting the freshest produce because conventional produce is harvested before ripening and travels long distances (hello, carbon emissions) to get to your grocery store and the quality of the food declines the more time that passes between when picked and when it makes it to your table.

Frozen fruits and veggies can be a great option if you can't buy them locally, because they are picked at the peak of ripeness and then blanched and flash-frozen to remove bacteria and lock in their essential vitamins and nutrients. The faster they are frozen after picking, the more nutrients they generally keep. Frozen fruit and veggies can last for several months if stored properly in your freezer, while fresh last only a few days to a week or so.

Canned vegetables can lose some of their vitamin C in the heating process during canning, but when they are handled and canned quickly, the majority of nutrients are locked in and maintained. That means canned veggies can have the same if not more nutrients than fresh veggies and the levels of these nutrients remain the same even after one or two of storage.

Read the labels on cans to steer clear of BPA (or try products packaged in jars) and opt for low or no-sodium versions.

And lastly, when choosing frozen veggies or fruit, the only ingredient listed should be the veggie or fruit—nothing else.

Tips for Picking Fresh Produce

- **Avocados.** Feel for firm flesh. Toss back avocados with sunken mushy spots. They should not rattle when shaken, that's a sign the pit has pulled away from dried out flesh. Buy a little under ripe (firmer) if you don't plan on using them right away. Seal them in a paper bag to ripen them quickly.

- **Berries.** Flip the cartons over and look for juice stains. That means they are over ripe.

- **Kale.** The smaller the leaves, the more tender the kale. Avoid wilted foliage with discolored spots. You want moist leaves with a dark blue-green color. Before you serve kale, rinse well and massage with your hands for a couple of minutes to soften the fibrous leaves.

- **Peaches.** Look for well-colored fruit with no green spots. The flesh should yield slightly when lightly pressed and should have a fragrant aroma.

- **Tomatoes.** Look for tomatoes that are firm and heavy for their size. They should have a sweet tomato aroma. Don't store tomatoes in the refrigerator—it zaps the flavor. Keep them in a bowl on your counter away from sunlight.

Tips For Storing Produce

- All vegetables, except those of the root variety, in the refrigerator until you need them.

- All fruits except berries, including tomatoes and avocados, at room temperature away from direct light.

- All cut fruits and vegetables with a squeeze of lemon juice on them and in an airtight container. Cut produce rapidly oxidizes and vitamin C, an antioxidant, slows decay.

- All herbs (with their amazing phytonutrients) wrapped loosely in plastic and placed in the warmest part of the fridge (the door works well). Do not wrap the herbs tightly or the trapped moisture may cause them to mold prematurely. Or, chop and freeze them in an ice cube tray with water.

Produce for Every Season

	WINTER	SPRING	SUMMER	FALL
Apples	O		O	O
Artichokes			O	
Asparagus		O		
Beans			O	O
Beets		O	O	O
Blackberries			O	
Blueberries			O	
Boysenberries			O	
Broccoli/Broccolini			O	O
Brussels Sprouts	O			
Cabbage	O		O	O
Carrots	O		O	O
Cauliflower			O	O
Celery	O	O	O	O
Cherries			O	O
Cucumber			O	O
Eggplant			O	O
Escarole	O			
Figs			O	
Fennel	O			
Garlic			O	O
Greens (arugula, lettuce, kale, spinach, swiss chard)	O	O	O	O
Leeks	O			
Melons			O	O
Nectarines			O	
Onions	O		O	O
Parsnips	O			
Peaches			O	
Pears				O
Peas		O	O	O
Peppers		O	O	O
Plums				O
Pomegranates	O			
Potatoes (white and sweet)	O		O	O
Pumpkin	O			O
Radicchio	O			
Radishes	O		O	
Raspberries			O	
Rhubarb		O		
Spring onions		O		
Strawberries		O	O	
Summer squash			O	O
Sweet corn			O	
Tomatoes			O	O
Turnips	O		O	O
Watermelon			O	
Winter squash	O			O
Zucchini				O

Meat & Poultry Tips

Whole Foods' meat and fish counters use a numeric rating system that tells you about the treatment of the animal and the quality of the product. Other stores may use a similar system to tell you more about what you're buying so you can make informed choices.

Look for leaner options when it comes to meat and poultry. Removing the skin from chicken (whether the butcher does it or you do before you cook it) shaves fat and calories. Here are a few of my favorite cuts of meat:

- Filet mignon
- Rib-eye
- Flank steak
- Sirloin tip side steak
- Top round roast and steak
- Bottom round roast and steak
- Top sirloin steak
- Eye of round roast or steak

There are also a few terms you want to look for on the labels or at the meat counter or on your dairy products:

- **Choice or Select.** Cuts of beef that usually have less fat than cuts labeled Prime. If you're unsure or there's no label, look for cuts with the least amount of visible fat (marbling).

- **Free-Range.** This designation means that the birds have been allowed access to the outdoors. However, there are no requirements for the amount of time the birds have access to the outside or the quality or size of the area. There are also no regulations on the supplemental feed that is given to the birds.

- **Grass-Fed.** Beef from cattle that has been raised exclusively on grass has less saturated fat and more nutrients that grain-finished beef. USDA grass-fed beef has only has a grass diet and access to pasture year-round. The program is voluntary, however, without third-party verification. Labels that read "100% grass-fed" or "grass-finished" and verified by a third party, such as the American Grass-Fed Association, will guarantee the cows have only been fed grass or hay.

- **Natural.** The USDA defines "natural" and "all-natural" food products as those that are minimally processed and contain no artificial ingredients. These terms do not mean that a product is organic, free of GMOs, or even ethically raised.

- **Organic.** USDA-certification for organic meat forbids the use of growth hormones, antibiotics, genetically modified feed, or animal by-products in raising the livestock. Beyond those practices, it does not address the treatment of the animals.

- **Pastured.** Typically applies to poultry (including the eggs of laying hens) and pork, and is used to emphasize that the animals have been raised primarily outdoors on live pasture where they can dig or peck for insects, seeds, and whatever else they can catch. If possible, 100% pasture-raised animals are superior, as they are allowed to roam freely and forage on the ground as they were meant to, and are not given a feed of soy, corn, or other grains. The best source for this type of meat and eggs is local farmers.

- **No Antibiotics.** Producers must submit documentation that the cattle were not administered any antibiotics to label their beef "raised without antibiotics," but there isn't any third-party verification or testing.

Fish & Seafood Tips

Fish and seafood can be great sources of omega-3s and protein. But you want to know what you're buying. Mislabeling practices on fish can not only set you up to be ripped off, but can also harm your health.

Use these tips to make sure you get what you bought or ordered:

1. **Buy direct from the fisherman at a farmer's market or pier** if you can. Farmer's markets usually have a fish stand where you can buy locally caught fish.

2. **Trace the species of the fish** bought through some grocery chains like Wegmans and Whole Foods and at hundreds of restaurants through companies like Trace Register and Trace and Trust. When you order fish, enter the ID number that comes with it into www.traceandtrust.com to get the deets on the species.

3. **Stick with safer bets** like mahi mahi, flounder and tilapia. They are the least likely to be mislabeled in restaurants. Salmon is also less likely to be mislabeled although it may be called wild when it's farmed.

4. **Go canned for fish like salmon or tuna.** Tests so far haven't found issues and the potential for mislabeling is lower because canned fish passes through fewer hands than fresh fish.

5. **Ask your fishmonger, the waiter or even the chef where they source their fish.**

Grocery Shopping Tips

1. **Buy in bulk.** Many Costcos are now offering more organic selections and you save money by buying bigger quantities of things you use often. Sam's Club is another bulk store that may be in your area. Just beware of over-purchasing perishable items that can go to waste before you can use all of them. Sometimes I take a friend with me and we split items such as cheese, avocados, lemons and greens.

2. **Buy online.** Amazon.com. Wisechoice.com, Thrive.com and other websites offer items you may not be able to find in your local grocery stores. Plus, it gets shipped right to your door—often in just a day or two.

3. **Don't go on an empty stomach.** Everything will sound good and you'll fill your cart with stuff you probably wouldn't otherwise. A recent Cornell University study showed that hungry grocery shoppers purchased 31 percent more high-calorie foods than those who had snacked before hitting the aisles.

4. **Stay on the outside perimeter of the store for the most part.** That's where the real foods are. Real food doesn't have a label. By definition, if a food has a label, it's been processed in some way. Real food spoils, which is a good thing. If bacteria can digest it, so can you.

5. **Make a list and take it with you.** That way you don't end up with stuff you don't need and you don't forget the stuff that you do need. I use a mobile app to make my list. This app also allows me to email the list to others, which is great when someone else has to do the shopping!

Breakfast

**Rise and shine, beautiful.
It's going to be a great day!**

You're probably used to breakfast staples like cereal, oats, pancakes, bagels or toast and other starchy breakfast foods. But with the advice I share in *Flat & Happy: Getting a Flat Belly & Happy Body for Life* to steer clear of starchy carbs in the morning to help stabilize your insulin and blood sugar, the breakfast section in this guide focuses more heavily on protein, fat and vegetables. Changing over to some of these types of options for breakfast might take some getting used to, but once you get a load of how you feel and how your body responds, I'll bet you never want to go back to the old way of thinking about breakfast.

With that being said, there are times when I want some of the old standards for breakfast or I'm cooking for people who don't eat like I do, so I've included some additional options that are still on the healthy side at the end of the section.

Kale, Sausage & Leek Frittata

SERVES 8

- ½   pound sausage (flavor of your choice), casings removed, crumbled
- 2   cups green curly kale leaves, washed and patted dry, chopped
- –   unsalted grass-fed butter or avocado oil
- 3   medium leeks (about 2 cups), trimmed, quartered lengthwise, washed well and sliced, using white and green parts
- 8   large organic omega-3 eggs
- 4   tbsp liquid egg whites
- ⅓   cup low-fat dairy milk or other milk of choice (try the Almond Milk, see Other Recipes section)
- ¼   cup fresh flat-leaf parsley, chopped + additional for garnish
- ½   tsp freshly ground black pepper
- ½   tsp sea salt
- –   couple dashes of Tabasco or other hot chili sauce

BROWN the crumbled sausage in a large, oven-safe sauté pan over medium-high heat. Make sure the sausage is not crowded in the pan (pieces should not touch) so that it will brown rather than steam. Season with a pinch salt and pepper. Drain the browned sausage and set aside.

ADD chopped leeks and kale to the pan, adding a bit of butter or cooking oil as needed. Sauté over low to medium-low heat until softened, about 8 to 10 minutes. Do not allow the leeks to brown as they will develop a bitter taste.

MIX eggs, milk, salt, black pepper, parsley and Tabasco or chili sauce in a small bowl and beat until foamy.

RETURN sausage to the pan and stir to mix thoroughly. Raise heat to medium-high and cook for 1 to 2 minutes. Evenly spread vegetables and sausage across the pan, and then mix eggs one last time and quickly pour over vegetable mixture in the pan. Gently shake or tilt the pan to even out the level of the eggs in the pan if necessary. Cook at medium-high heat for about 3 minutes, and then reduce heat to medium-low and cook until the edges are crisp and the top is beginning to firm up, about 10 minutes. Keep tilting the pan so the liquid fills in underneath (makes it cook faster and more evenly).

PLACE an oven rack at a high-middle position and turn on the oven broiler to low. Once most of the frittata is cooked, but there is still a bit of liquid visible on top, turn off the burner and transfer the pan to the oven under a broiler. Broil for approximately 4 minutes, or until the top of the frittata is puffed up and golden.

REMOVE from the oven and let cool for approximately 5 minutes. Slide a thin, flexible spatula between the edges of the frittata and the pan, all the way around, and then tilt the pan, with the spatula underneath the leading edge of the frittata. Gently slide the frittata out onto the cutting board. Garnish with fresh chopped parsley or herb of choice.

CUT into 8 pieces and serve warm or at room temperature.

TIP! Refrigerate or freeze the extras and you've got more meals already prepared for the coming week.

Feta, Green Onion & Asparagus Frittata

SERVES 4

6	large organic omega-3 eggs + 2 large egg whites
¼	tsp sea salt
¼	tsp freshly ground black pepper
–	unsalted grass-fed butter or avocado oil
1	cup low-fat dairy milk or other milk of choice
8	asparagus spears, woody ends removed and cut into ½-inch pieces
¼	cup shallots, thinly sliced
3	tbsp green onions, chopped
2	ounces crumbled feta cheese (or goat cheese)

TURN oven on low broil and set rack in the middle.

WHISK eggs, egg whites, salt, pepper and milk together well.

HEAT a 9-inch oven-safe sauté pan over medium heat and melt cooking fat. Sauté asparagus and shallot for a couple of minutes until tender.

POUR in egg mixture and add cheese, allowing it to cook at medium heat for about 3 minutes, then reduce heat to medium-low and cook until the edges are crisp and the top begins to firm up, about 10 minutes. Keep tilting the pan so the liquid fills in underneath to help it cook faster and more evenly.

TURN off burner and transfer the pan to the oven once most of the fritatta is cooked, but there is still a bit of liquid visible on top. Broil for approximately 4 minutes, or until the top of the frittata is puffed up and golden.

REMOVE from the oven and allow to cool in the pan for approximately 5 minutes. Slide a thin, flexible spatula between the edges of the frittata and the pan, all the way around, and then tilt the pan, with the spatula underneath the leading edge of the frittata, and gently slide the frittata out onto the cutting board.

SPRINKLE with green onion and cut into 4 pieces. Serve warm or at room temperature.

Asparagus & Mushroom Scramble

SERVES 1

2	omega-3, organic brown eggs
2	tbsp liquid egg whites
–	unsalted grass-fed butter or avocado oil
3	asparagus spears, woody ends removed and cut into ½-inch pieces
5	cremini mushrooms, stems removed and sliced
1	tbsp grated Parmesan or Pecorino Romano cheese

WHISK eggs, egg whites, salt and pepper together well in a bowl and set aside.

HEAT cooking fat in a sauté pan over medium heat and add mushrooms and asparagus to soften and cook, about 4 minutes.

POUR egg mixture over vegetables. Add cheese. Allow eggs to cook completely, stirring occasionally.

Spinach Avocado Pesto Scramble

SERVES 1

- 2 organic omega-3 eggs
- 2 tbsp liquid egg whites
- 2 cups baby spinach
- — unsalted grass-fed butter or avocado oil
- 2 tbsp Spinach Avocado Pesto (see Other Recipes section)
- — pinch of sea salt
- — freshly ground black pepper

WHISK eggs, egg whites, salt and pepper together well in a bowl and set aside.

HEAT cooking fat in a sauté pan over medium heat and add spinach to wilt down, about 2 to 3 minutes.

POUR egg mixture over spinach. Stir to incorporate. When eggs are almost done, add pesto and finish cooking, stirring occasionally.

Breakfast Bowl

SERVES 1

- 1 omega-3, organic eggs
- 2 cups baby or curly green kale (use baby spinach if you prefer)
- — pinch of sea salt
- 1 tsp unsalted grass-fed butter or avocado oil

Optional
- — ¼ cup cooked quinoa (sub in ½ cup pre-made roasted sweet potato, cauliflower or parsnips if desired)

COOK the quinoa according to package directions and set aside. You could also use reheated leftovers.

DE-STEM and chop the kale if using curly green variety (baby kale needs no prep). Heat cooking fat in a non-stick sauté pan and add kale, stirring occasionally until softened and bright green. Add to bowl. Allow pan to cool a little.

MELT cooking fat over medium low heat. Add eggs to pan and cook gently on both sides until egg whites are fully cooked, but yolks are still runny.

ADD quinoa (or other starch) to bowl, and top with eggs.

TIP! Prepare pesto ahead of time and use the leftovers on spaghetti squash or zucchini noodles.

Avocado Breakfast Bake

SERVES 1

- 1 ripe avocado, halved, pit removed
- 2 large, organic omega-3 eggs
- – pinch of sea salt
- – freshly ground black pepper
- – toppings of choice

PREHEAT oven to 350 degrees. Put avocado halves open side up in a large baking dish. If they are small avocados, scoop out a little of the extra flesh to make more room for the egg.

CRACK one egg in each avocado half and sprinkle with salt and pepper. Place on middle oven rack and bake for 15 to 20 minutes or until egg is at desired level of doneness.

SPRINKLE with toppings of choice: feta and green onions, salsa and fresh cilantro, a few bacon crumbles ... whatever you like. Serve hot.

> **TIP!** Poaching eggs is quick and easy. It takes only about 4 minutes in a pan, or just over a minute in the microwave. Check Amazon.com for inexpensive microwave poachers.

Roasted Asparagus & Arugula Breakfast Salad

SERVES 4

- 1 pound asparagus spears, woody ends trimmed
- 3 tbsp extra-virgin olive oil, divided
- ½ tsp freshly ground black pepper
- ¼ tsp sea salt, divided
- 3 tbsp minced shallots
- 2 tbsp fresh lemon juice
- 2 tsp chopped fresh tarragon
- 1 5-ounce package fresh baby arugula
- 1 tbsp white wine vinegar
- 4 large, organic omega-3 eggs

PREHEAT oven to 425 degrees.

PLACE asparagus on baking sheet. Drizzle with 2 tsp oil; sprinkle with ¼ tsp pepper and ⅛ tsp salt. Toss gently to coat; arrange in a single layer. Bake for 8 to 10 minutes or until crisp-tender.

PLACE remaining oil, ⅛ tsp pepper, remaining ⅛ tsp salt, shallots, vinegar, juice and tarragon in a large bowl; stir well with a whisk. Add arugula and toss gently to coat. Place about 1½ cups arugula mixture on each of 4 plates. Top each serving with ¼ of the asparagus.

POACH eggs and place one on each salad. Sprinkle with remaining pepper.

NUTRITION FACTS

PER SERVING: 261 CALORIES, 15.3G FAT, 11.9G PROTEIN, 19.8G CARBS, 3.6G FIBER, 327MG SODIUM

Potato, Kale & Sausage Hash

SERVES 6

1	small bag unpeeled baby potatoes, cut in half or quarters so they are bite-sized
1	pound sausage (flavor of choice), casing removed, crumbled
¾	cup chopped yellow or red onion
1	chopped red, yellow or green bell pepper
3	leaves chopped curly green kale, de-stemmed
3	garlic cloves, minced
–	juice of ½ lemon
¼	cup flat leaf parsley, chopped
6	large organic omega-3 eggs
–	unsalted grass-fed butter or avocado oil
–	extra-virgin olive oil
1½	tbsp ground cumin
1	tsp smoked paprika
–	sea salt and freshly ground black pepper

PREHEAT oven to 450 degrees. Spread potatoes out on foil-lined baking sheets and mist with olive oil. Sprinkle with salt and pepper, and bake for 25 to 30 minutes until crisp/tender.

BROWN the sausage in a large sauté pan over medium-high heat. Break up the sausage into bite-sized chunks so it cooks evenly. Season with salt and pepper. Remove the sausage from pan and place on a towel-lined plate, or in a strainer to drain off the grease.

ADD onions and peppers to the pan and cook over medium heat until translucent. You may need to add a little oil, but the grease from the sausage should be enough. Add garlic and stir for 1 to 2 minutes.

ADD roasted potatoes to the onions, pepper and garlic mixture. Add in cumin and paprika and stir to make sure the mixture is seasoned well. If you need to add a little more than called for, go ahead to your taste. Add the lemon juice and black pepper to taste.

ADD the browned sausage and chopped kale into the mixture and let warm up for a couple of minutes, stirring to combine. Remove from heat.

HEAT a small sauté pan over medium low heat, and add butter or oil to the pan. Once warmed, add eggs to the pan and let cook on one side for about 2 to 3 minutes. Turn and cook another minute or so (don't overcook …you want the yolks to be runny!)

PLATE the hash and top with the egg and fresh parsley.

Chicken & Sweet Potato Hash

SERVES 4

- 1 pinch sea salt
- 2 large boneless, skinless chicken breasts (or whole roasted chicken from the store)
- 2 tsp extra-virgin olive oil
- 1¼ pound jeweled sweet potatoes, peeled and cut into ¼-inch pieces
- 1 cup red onion, halved and thinly sliced
- ½ tsp smoked paprika + additional for garnish
- ½ tsp ground cumin
- ¼ tsp sea salt
- ¼ cup fresh cilantro, finely chopped
- 4 large organic omega-3 eggs

SEASON a large pot of water with a pinch of salt and bring to a simmer.

ADD chicken, cover and simmer for about 8 to 10 minutes, or until chicken is cooked through. Remove from pot and set aside until cool enough to handle.

SHRED or chop chicken and set aside. If you are using store-bought chicken, you can skip the first two steps and just shred your chicken.

HEAT oil on medium in a large sauté pan.

ADD potatoes and onion, stirring occasionally until potato is just tender, about 15 minutes.

FOLD chicken gently into potato mixture and cook, stirring occasionally until potatoes and chicken are browned, about 5 to 10 minutes. Stir in paprika, cumin, salt and cilantro.

SERVE with 1 egg and additional paprika on top.

NUTRITIONAL FACTS

PER SERVING (1¼ CUPS HASH AND 1 EGG): 294 CALORIES, 10G FAT, 14G CARBS, 3G FIBER, 5G SUGARS, 35G PROTEIN, 368MG SODIUM

Smoked Salmon Avocado Toast

SERVES 1

- ½ ripe avocado, mashed
- 1 large slice smoked salmon
- 1 slice whole grain or seed bread
- — freshly ground black pepper

TOAST bread and top with mashed avocado, salmon and pepper. Serve immediately.

Basic Protein Pancakes

MAKES 4 TO 5 PANCAKES

- ½ cup quick cooking oatmeal
- ½ cup liquid egg whites
- ½ large banana
- ¼ tsp ground cinnamon
- ½ tsp lemon or orange zest
- 1 tbsp extra-virgin olive oil
- ¼ tsp ground nutmeg
- – olive oil or coconut oil cooking spray

BLEND all ingredients together in a blender or food processor until incorporated (but don't over mix).

HEAT griddle pan over medium heat. Mist with cooking spray and drop ⅓ cup batter onto pan to form 4 pancakes. Let sit for about 2 minutes until top starts to bubble and bottom is golden brown. Flip and let cook another 2 minutes. Place on a plate while you make the remaining pancakes.

SERVE hot with fresh fruit and/or butter.

NUTRITION FACTS

PER SERVING (1 PANCAKE): 84 CALORIES, 1G FAT, 110MG SODIUM, 10G CARBS, 1G SUGAR, 4G PROTEIN

TIP! Store leftover pancakes 4 to a sandwich bag in the freezer and pull out a bag when needed. These also make for a great dessert with a little almond butter.

Blood Orange Zucchini Pancakes

MAKES 22 TO 24 PANCAKES

- 3 cups oats, ground to flour in food processor (or just use oat flour)
- 3 organic omega-3 eggs
- 2 cups unsweetened organic almond or soy milk
- 2 tbsp blood orange olive oil
- – juice of 1 orange + the zest of that orange
- 2 medium zucchini, finely grated
- 2 tsp baking soda
- 2 tbsp ground cinnamon
- 1 tsp ground all spice
- 1 tsp real vanilla extract
- ¼ tsp sea salt
- 4 medium bananas
- – olive oil or coconut oil cooking spray

PUREÉ bananas in a blender or food processor and set aside. Grate zucchini and squeeze gently to remove some of the excess moisture.

GRIND oats into rough flour in food processor and pour into a bowl. Or, if using pre-ground oat floor, add to your bowl. Add cinnamon, all spice, baking soda, salt and stir to combine.

MIX olive oil, orange juice, orange zest, vanilla, eggs, milk, banana and zucchini together in a separate bowl.

ADD wet ingredients to dry ingredients and stir until fully incorporated, but don't over mix.

HEAT a griddle pan over medium heat. Spray with cooking spray and drop ⅓ cup of batter onto pan to make 4 pancakes. Let cook for about 2 minutes until top starts to bubble and bottom is golden brown. Flip and let cook another 1 to 2 minutes. Place on a plate and make the other pancakes.

SERVE immediately with fresh fruit and/or butter (you won't need syrup with these).

Buckwheat Banana Pancakes

MAKES 12 TO 14 PANCAKES

Buckwheat is a fruit seed that is related to rhubarb and sorrel. It's a good substitute to grains for people who are sensitive to wheat or other grains that contain protein glutens and oatmeal for those who are sensitive to it. Buckwheat flour is darker and has more texture than regular flour, so your pancakes will turn out pretty dark and a little grainy—not like the traditional pancakes you may be used to. But once you bite into these fluffy cakes, you'll be hooked!

- 2½ cups organic buckwheat flour
- 2 tsp baking soda
- 1 tsp sea salt
- 2 cups unsweetened organic almond or soy milk
- 4 small bananas
- 1 tbsp real vanilla extract
- 1 tbsp ground cinnamon
- 2 organic omega-3 eggs
- 2 tbsp extra-virgin olive oil
- – olive oil or coconut oil cooking spray

PUREÉ bananas in a blender or food processor and set aside.

MIX together flour, baking soda, cinnamon and salt in a medium-sized mixing bowl.

BEAT together the milk, eggs, vanilla, bananas and olive oil in a separate mixing bowl. Once thoroughly mixed, add liquid mixture to dry mixture. Stir until the batter is mostly smooth (don't over mix). Set aside for 10 minutes to allow the flour to fully absorb the liquid ingredients.

HEAT a griddle pan over medium heat. Spray with cooking spray and drop ⅓ cup of batter onto pan to make 4 pancakes. Let cook for about 2 minutes until top starts to bubble and bottom is golden brown. Flip and let cook another 1 to 2 minutes. Place on a plate and make the other pancakes.

SERVE hot with butter, almond butter or berries.

Coconut Berry Baked Oatmeal

SERVES 4 TO 6

- 2 tbsp unsalted grass-fed butter
- 2 cups gluten-free rolled oats
- 1 tsp baking powder
- 2 tsp ground cinnamon
- 1 tsp ground ginger
- ½ tsp sea salt
- ⅓ cup pecans, coarsely chopped
- ⅓ thick-shredded coconut
- ½ cups mixed berries, fresh or frozen
- 1 large organic omega-3 egg
- ⅓ cup pure maple syrup or organic honey
- 2 tsp real vanilla extract
- 2 cups milk of your choice

Optional
- – plain Greek yogurt or mascarpone cheese

PREHEAT oven to 375 degrees with oven rack in the top third of the oven. Place butter in a deep casserole dish or 8-inch square baking dish and set the dish in the oven. Allow to heat for about 3 minutes, or until the butter is melted. Remove dish from the oven.

MIX together oats, baking powder, cinnamon, ginger and salt while the butter is melting. Pour into the baking dish, and toss the oats until they are coated with butter. Stir in pecans and coconut, mixing well, then toss in berries. Make sure blueberries are evenly scattered around the dish.

WHISK together the egg, maple syrup or honey and vanilla in the same bowl. Mix until well combined, and then stir in the milk. Slowly and evenly pour over the oats.

BAKE 35 to 45 minutes, or until the top turns gently golden and the edges are bubbling. Cool a few minutes before serving. Top with yogurt or mascarpone cheese if desired.

NUTRITION FACTS

PER SERVING: 475 CALORIES, 23G FAT
57G CARBS, 530MG SODIUM, 7G FIBER,
13G PROTEIN, 85MG CHOLESTEROL

Warm & Nutty Cinnamon Quinoa

SERVES 4

1	cup unsweetened almond or coconut milk
½	cup water
1	cup organic quinoa (rinsed); red, or white/buff colored
2	cups fresh berries, organic preferred
½	tsp ground cinnamon
⅓	cup pecans or almonds, coarsely chopped and toasted

COMBINE milk, water and quinoa in a medium saucepan.

BRING to a boil over high heat then reduce heat to medium-low. Cover and simmer 15 minutes or until most of the liquid is absorbed.

TURN off heat; let stand covered 5 minutes.

TOAST nuts in a 350-degree oven for 5 to 6 minutes or in a dry sauté pan over medium heat for 3 minutes.

STIR blackberries and cinnamon into quinoa. Transfer to bowls and top with nuts.

Savory Oatmeal

SERVES 1

½	cup gluten-free thick rolled oats (not instant); sub steel cut oats if you prefer
1	cup water
–	pinch of sea salt
–	pinch of freshly ground black pepper
1	large handful baby spinach
¼	cup shredded cheese (smoked gouda or pepper jack works well for flavor)
1	large organic omega-3 egg
4	tbsp liquid egg whites

BRING oats, salt, pepper and water to a boil, then reduce heat to simmer for 8 to 10 minutes, or until oats are tender.

PUT egg and egg whites in microwave egg poacher and cook for 1 minute + 10 to 15 seconds until egg an egg whites are done to your liking. You could also fry 2 eggs if you prefer.

STIR spinach into oatmeal until wilted, and then add cheese until melted.

SPOON oats mixture into a bowl and top with eggs. Sprinkle with freshly ground black pepper and serve immediately.

TIP! If you like oats in the morning, try the steel-cut variety or quinoa. Both are still a whole grain and take longer to break down and digest, which means they don't spike insulin as much as rolled oats will.

Smoothies

In life, much like smoothies, you get out what you put in.

Smoothies can be an easy way to get in the recommended 6 to 10 servings of vegetables, greens and fruit per day. Plus, they're simple to make and perfect when you need something on the go ('cause we're all so damn busy!).

These smoothie recipes are intended to be meals—meaning they are 250+ calories. Adding protein powder is optional, but using it will definitely make the smoothie a more complete meal. One of my favorite protien powders is *Upgraded Self's* collagen protein (upgradedself.com). There are a lot of high-quality, plant-based protein powders on the market too. Look for a low-carb and low-sugar on the label.

Directions (for all smoothies)
Toss all ingredients in a blender and blend until smooth—about 1 minute. Enjoy!

Lemony Green Smoothie

SERVES 1

2	large handfuls baby spinach
2	celery stalks, chopped roughly
6	cucumber slices, halved
½	ripe avocado
–	small handful fresh parsley
–	juice of 1 lemon
8	chunks frozen pineapple
1	to 2 tbsp collagen protein or 1 to 2 scoops plant-based protein powder
1	cup filtered water + more for desired consistency

Blueberry Kale Smoothie

SERVES 1

½	cup blueberries
1	cup kale (baby kale works best)
½	large frozen banana
½	cup unsweetened almond or coconut milk
1	to 2 tbsp collagen protein or 1 to 2 scoops plant-based protein powder

Greens & Beans Smoothie

SERVES 2

2	cups unsweetened almond or coconut milk
1	to 2 tbsp collagen protein or 1 to 2 scoops plant-based protein powder
1	cup frozen peach or mango slices
½	ripe avocado
½	cup canned cannelini beans, rinsed and drained
1½	cups baby spinach
1	tbsp organic honey
¼	cup fresh basil leaves
2	tsp fresh ginger, grated

Vanilla Latte Energizer Smoothie

SERVES 1   (d) (g)

- 1 to 2 tbsp collagen protein or 1 to 2 scoops plant-based protein powder
- ½ cup brewed strong coffee or espresso
- 1 tsp organic honey
- 1 tsp good vanilla extract
- ½ tsp cinnamon
- – ice cubes

Almond Butter Smoothie

SERVES 1   (d) (g)

- 1 cup unsweetened almond milk
- 1 tbsp organic cacao powder
- 1½ tbsp organic almond butter (preferably raw)
- 1 pitted medjool date
- – ice cubes

Banana Blackberry Smoothie

SERVES 1   (d) (g)

- ⅔ cup fresh or frozen blackberries
- ½ fresh or frozen banana
- ¼ tbsp organic honey
- ⅛ tsp real vanilla extract
- – crushed ice
- 1 cup unsweetened almond or coconut milk

TIP! The Banana Blackberry Smoothie is a good option for the afternoon or a refreshing dessert. It's not the best option for breakfast because of the fruit content and the fact that it doesn't have much protein or healthy fat.

Sides

Don't ever allow yourself to be a side dish in somebody's life. Insist on being the main course.

I love side dishes. Sometimes even more than the main part of the meal. All of the recipes in this section are easy to make and big on flavor.

You'll notice that veggies are the star in most of these sides, making it even easier to get in your 6 to 10 servings a day.

Balsamic & Parmesan Roasted Cauliflower

SERVES 4

- 8 cups sliced cauliflower florets (about 1 large head)
- 2 tbsp olive oil or avocado oil
- 1 tsp dried marjoram
- ¼ cup Parmesan cheese, finely shredded
- 2 tbsp balsamic vinegar
- ¼ tsp sea salt
- – freshly ground black pepper to taste

PREHEAT oven to 450 degrees.

PREPARE cauliflower florets by slicing off the thick stem and removing outer leaves. With the head upside down and holding a knife at a 45-degree angle, slice into the smaller stems with a circular motion, removing the "plug" from the center of the head. Break or cut florets into 1-inch thick pieces.

TOSS cauliflower, oil, marjoram, salt and pepper in a large bowl. Spread on a large, foil-lined rimmed baking sheet and roast until starting to soften and brown on the bottom, 15 to 20 minutes. Toss the cauliflower with vinegar and sprinkle with cheese. Return to the oven and roast until the cheese is melted and any moisture has evaporated, 5 to 10 minutes more.

NUTRITION FACTS

PER SERVING (ABOUT 1 CUP): 149 CALORIES, 10G FAT (3 G SAT, 6G MONO), 7MG CHOLESTEROL, 10G CARBS, 7G PROTEIN, 4G FIBE,; 364MG SODIUM, 490MG POTASSIUM

Cauliflower Rice (3 Ways)

SERVES 4

Basic Rice

- 1 small head cauliflower, cut into florets
- 2 tsp ghee or unsalted grass-fed butter
- 1 tsp cold-pressed sesame oil
- ½ cup yellow onion, diced
- 1 garlic clove, minced
- ¼ cup water
- ¾ tsp sea salt

"RICE" the cauliflower using a food processor with a grating attachment or a box grater. Pick out any large fragments that didn't get shredded and save for another use.

MELT the ghee or butter and sesame oil in a large sauté pan over medium heat. Add the onion and garlic and sauté for 5 minutes, until the onion has softened. Add the cauliflower to the pan and sauté for 5 minutes.

ADD the water and salt and increase the heat to medium-high. Cook for 15 minutes, until the cauliflower is tender and the liquid has been absorbed.

Coconut, Cilantro & Lime Rice

- 1 small head cauliflower, cut into florets
- 1 tsp coconut oil
- 1 tbsp fresh lime juice
- 2 tsp organic honey
- ¼ cup fresh cilantro, chopped
- ¼ cup full-fat coconut milk
- ¼ cup water
- ¾ tsp sea salt

"RICE" the cauliflower using a food processor with a grating attachment or a box grater. Pick out any large fragments that didn't get shredded and save for another use.

MELT the coconut oil in a large sauté pan over medium heat. Add the cauliflower to the pan and sauté for 5 minutes.

ADD the remaining ingredients and cook for 15 minutes, until the cauliflower is tender and the liquid has been absorbed.

Saffron Rice

- 1 small head cauliflower, cut into florets
- 2 tsp ghee or unsalted grass-fed butter
- ¼ cup low-sodium chicken stock or broth
- ½ tsp saffron threads
- ½ cup yellow onion, diced
- 1 garlic clove, minced
- 1 tsp garam masala
- ¼ cup peas
- ¼ cup water
- ¾ tsp sea salt

"RICE" the cauliflower using a food processor with a grating attachment or a box grater. Pick out any large fragments that didn't get shredded and save for another use.

BRING the chicken stock to a boil in a small saucepan, then add the saffron. Cover and remove from the heat.

MELT the ghee or butter in a large sauté pan over medium heat. Add the cauliflower to the pan and continue to sauté over medium heat for 5 minutes. Add the onion, garlic, garam masala, and salt and sauté for 5 minutes, until the onion has softened.

POUR in the saffron broth and the peas and increase the heat to medium-high. Cook for 15 minutes, until the cauliflower is tender and the liquid has been absorbed.

Garlic & Sage Spaghetti Squash

SERVES 4

1	medium to large spaghetti squash, halved, seeds removed
2	tbsp olive oil, divided
¼	cup Parmesan cheese, grated
1	tbsp fresh sage, chopped
¼	tsp sea salt
–	freshly ground black pepper to taste

PREHEAT oven to 400 degrees. Brush sides of cut squash with 1 tbsp olive oil and place cut side down on baking sheet.

ROAST squash until fork-tender, about 45 to 50 minutes. Remove from oven and let cool for 10 minutes.

SCRAPE squash with a fork to remove flesh in long strands. Toss squash strands with remaining oil, Parmesan and sage. Season with salt and pepper.

NUTRITION FACTS

PER SERVING (ABOUT 1 CUP):
170 CALORIES, 7G FAT, 10G CARBS,
2G FIBER, 4G PROTEIN

Mashed Squash with Caramelized Onions

SERVES 6

2	large butternut squashes, peeled, halved and seeded
1	head garlic, unpeeled
3	medium white onions, diced
1½	tsp sherry vinegar
¼	cup olive oil
½	tsp sea salt
–	freshly ground black pepper to taste

PREHEAT oven to 375 degrees. Line a baking sheet with foil for an easy clean up. Mist cut side of squash with olive oil. Sprinkle on salt and pepper.

PLACE squash cut side down on the prepared pan. Bake until flesh is very tender, about 45 to 55 minutes.

HEAT oil in a large sauté pan over high heat. Add onions and salt; cook, stirring frequently, until the onions begin to brown, about 5 minutes. Reduce heat to medium low and cook, stirring frequently until onions are golden brown and very soft, about 15 minutes more. Stir in vinegar and pepper and cook a few more minutes. Remove from heat, cover and keep warm.

SCRAPE the squash into the pan when cool enough to handle. Return to medium-low heat and mash, stirring to incorporate the onions.

NUTRITION FACTS

PER SERVING (½ CUP): 181 CALORIES,
10G FAT (1G SATURATED), 24G CARBS,
7G SUGARS (0G ADDED), 2G PROTEIN,
4G FIBER, 202MG SODIUM

TIP! Most grocery stores sell pre-cut, cubed butternut squash. It can be real time and effort saver if you don't feel like peeling and preparing your squash.

Honey-Roasted Butternut Squash

SERVES 6

1	large butternut squash, halved and seeded
2	tbsp organic honey
1½	tbsp unsalted grass-fed butter
½	tsp sea salt
¼	tsp freshly ground black pepper
2	tbsp pecans, toasted and finely chopped
1	tbsp fresh flat-leaf parsley, minced

PREHEAT oven to 400 degrees. Place squash halves, cut sides up, on a foil-lined baking sheet. Place honey and butter in a microwave-safe bowl and microwave at high 30 seconds or until butter melts; stir to combine. Brush half of honey mixture over cut sides of squash; reserve remaining honey mixture. Sprinkle squash with salt and pepper. Bake for 1 hour or until tender.

PLACE squash, cut sides up, on cutting board. Halve squash lengthwise; cut each half crosswise into thirds. Place squash on a platter. Heat reserved butter mixture in microwave at high 20 seconds. Drizzle remaining butter mixture over squash; sprinkle evenly with pecans and parsley.

Rosemary Roasted Beets & Carrots

SERVES 2

½	pound beets, peeled and cut into ½-inch wedges
½	pound carrots, scrubbed and cut into 2-inch lengths (halved lengthwise if large)
⅛	cup red wine vinegar
1½	tbsp olive oil
1	sprig fresh rosemary
–	sea salt and freshly ground black pepper to taste

PREHEAT oven to 450 degrees. Toss the beets, carrots, vinegar, olive oil, rosemary and ¼ tsp each salt and pepper on a rimmed baking sheet.

ROAST, tossing once, until the vegetables are tender, about 30 to 35 minutes.

43 Sides

Brussels Sprouts with Pancetta & Sage

SERVES 8

1	large leek, white and light green part only, thinly sliced
8	cups Brussels sprouts, trimmed and halved
½	cup pancetta, chopped
2	tbsp fresh sage, finely chopped
¼	tbsp olive oil
½	tsp sea salt
½	freshly ground black pepper to taste

PREHEAT oven to 450 degrees. Rinse leek slices well to remove any grit, then pat dry. Combine with Brussels sprouts, pancetta, sage, olive oil, salt and pepper in a large roasting pan.

ROAST stirring once, until the Brussels sprouts are tender, about 18 to 20 minutes.

NUTRITION FACTS
PER SERVING (ABOUT 1 CUP): 109 CALORIES, 6G FAT, 5MG CHOLESTEROL, 4G PROTEIN, 3G FIBER, 0G ADDED SUGARS, 289MG SODIUM

Farro with Wild Mushrooms & Herbs

SERVES 4

1	cups dry semi-pearled farro
–	sea salt
1½	tbsp avocado or coconut oil
2	cups assorted fresh mushrooms (such as chantarelle, porcini, lobster or crimini), de-stemmed and cut into 1-inch pieces
½	cup low-sodium chicken broth
⅓	stick unsalted grass-fed butter, cut into ½-inch cubes + 1 tbsp if needed
¼	tbsp fresh flat-leaf parsley, chopped
1	tbsp fresh chives, chopped
1	tbsp fresh thyme, chopped
–	freshly ground black pepper to taste

COOK farro in boiling salted water until tender, about 20 minutes. Drain, let cool, and set aside.

HEAT 2 tbsp oil in a large sauté pan over medium-high heat until it shimmers (the oil needs to be very hot to crisp the mushrooms). Working in batches, add a single layer of mushrooms to pan. Cook, turning once, until crisp and cooked through, 4 to 5 minutes. Transfer to a plate; season with salt and pepper.

BRING broth to a simmer in a medium saucepan over medium heat. Add farro and cook, stirring often, until heated through.

SEASON farro with salt and pepper. Add butter and stir vigorously to combine and create a creamy texture.

ADD mushrooms, parsley, chives, and thyme; stir just to evenly incorporate. Serve immediately.

Risotto-Style Barley & Asparagus

SERVES 2

- ½ cup dry pearled barley
- 1½ cup + ½ cup low-sodium chicken or vegetable stock, divided
- 2 tsp avocado or coconut oil
- ½ small bunch asparagus, woody ends trimmed and cut diagonally into 1-inch pieces
- – sea salt and freshly ground black pepper to taste
- – zest of ½ lemon

ADD barley and 1½ cups stock to a medium saucepan. Bring to a boil, reduce heat to low, cover and simmer for about 45 minutes, or until tender and most of the liquid is absorbed. Fluff with a fork and set aside in saucepan.

HEAT oil in a second medium saucepan on medium-high. Add asparagus and zest and sauté for 2 minutes until tender-crisp. Add barley and remaining ½ cup stock and cook on medium, stirring constantly for 2 minutes. Season with salt and pepper. Any leftovers can be refrigerated in a covered container for 2 days.

NUTRITION FACTS
PER SERVING (½ CUP): 147 CALORIES, 3G FAT, 27G CARBS, 5G FIBER, 3G PROTEIN, 192MG SODIUM

Roasted Sweet Potatoes/Fries

SERVES 3

- 1 large jeweled sweet potato
- 1 tbsp olive, avocado or coconut oil
- 1 tsp sea salt
- – freshly ground black pepper
- 1 tbsp spice or spice combination of your choice (chipotle powder, smoked paprika, pumpkin pie spice, garam masala, etc)

PREHEAT oven to 450 degrees. Peel the sweet potato and cut off the ends. Cut the potato in half lengthwise and then, if it's very long, in half crosswise. Cut each piece into wedges or sticks.

PUT the sweet potatoes into a large bowl and add the oil. Mix well to combine. Sprinkle with salt, pepper and spices of your choice. Use your hands to mix well, so all pieces are coated with oil and spices.

SPREAD the sweet potatoes out in a single layer on a rimmed, foil-lined baking sheet.

BAKE for 15 minutes, then remove the baking sheet from the oven and turn over all of the sweet potato pieces. Bake for another 10 to 15 minutes, or until potatoes are well browned. Let cool for 5 minutes before serving.

Balsamic Vegetables

SERVES 6

- 2 tbsp balsamic vinegar
- 1 tsp Dijon mustard
- ½ cup avocado or coconut oil
- 3 garlic cloves, pressed or mashed
- 2 tsp fresh thyme, finely chopped
- 1 tsp fresh basil, finely shopped
- 2 large red onions, peeled and sliced into chunks
- 1 yellow bell pepper, cut into ½-inch wide strips
- 1 red bell pepper, cut into ½-inch wide strips
- 1 orange bell pepper, cut into ½-inch wide strips
- 1 large jeweled sweet potato, peeled, cut into ½-inch thick pieces
- 2 medium zucchini, cut into ⅓-inch thick rounds
- – sea salt and freshly ground black pepper to taste

WHISK vinegar and mustard in medium bowl. Gradually whisk in oil. Stir in garlic, thyme and basil. Season to taste with salt and pepper. Dressing can be made 1 day ahead. Keep covered and chilled.

PREHEAT oven to 450 degrees. Toss onions and vegetables in large bowl. Sprinkle with salt and pepper. Add dressing and toss to coat. Divide between two large, foil-lined, rimmed baking sheets. Roast until vegetables are tender and slightly brown around edges, about 35 minutes.

TIP! Store leftovers in the fridge for two to three days. Use for breakfasts, or put into salad with protein for healthy and fast lunch or dinner.

Roasted Fennel with Pears, Parmesan & Thyme

SERVES 4

- 1 medium fennel bulb
- 1 large firm, ripe pear (preferrably D'Anjou)
- 2 tbsp olive or avocado oil
- – sea salt
- – freshly ground black pepper
- 1 tsp fresh thyme, finely chopped
- 3 tbsp Parmesan cheese, freshly grated

PREHEAT oven to 500 degrees. Trim and reserve fennel fronds and cut off stalks. Quarter the bulb lengthwise and slice each quarter into three wedges. Peel, half and corepear and slice each half into 4 wedges.

LINE a large baking sheet with parchment paper. Arrange fennel around edges of baking sheet and pears toward center. Drizzle with oil and season with salt and pepper.

ROAST until fennel and pears are almost tender and bottoms look golden—about 15 minutes. Flip pieces, sprinkle with thyme and Parmesan, and return to oven until cheese is melted, about 2 minutes more. Transfer to a serving platter and garnish with the reserved fennel fronds.

NUTRITION FACTS
PER SERVING (½ CUP): 135 CALORIES, 9G FAT (2G SATURATED), 12G CARBS, 2.5G PROTEIN, 3.5G FIBER, 110MG SODIUM

Asparagus with Honey Orange Glaze

SERVES 4

Orange Citrus Glaze
- 1 large navel orange, zested and juiced (about ½ cup)
- 2 tbsp organic honey
- 2 tbsp fresh oregano, chopped
- 2 tbsp sherry vinegar
- – sea salt and freshly ground black pepper
- ½ cup extra-virgin olive oil

Asparagus
- 1 pound asparagus, woody ends trimmed
- 1 tbsp olive oil
- – sea salt and freshly ground black pepper
- – orange zest for garnish

WHISK together the orange juice, orange zest, honey, oregano, sherry vinegar, 2 large pinches of salt and a pinch of pepper. Slowly incorporate the olive oil to create an emulsion. Yield: about 1 cup

PLACE a rimmed baking sheet in the oven and preheat oven to 400 degrees.

TOSS the asparagus with the olive oil in a large bowl and sprinkle with salt and pepper. Add the asparagus to the hot baking sheet and cook until tender, about 10 minutes.

TRANSFER the asparagus to a serving platter. Drizzle with ⅓ cup of the orange citrus glaze and sprinkle with some orange zest.

Asparagus with Lemon & Pecorino

SERVES 4

- 1 bunch asparagus, woody ends trimmed
- 1 tsp olive oil
- 2 tsp zested lemon rind
- – sea salt
- – freshly ground black pepper
- 2 tbsp Pecorino Romano cheese, shaved

BRING a large pot of water to boil. Add asparagus, cook for 2 minutes or until crisp/tender. Drain.

HEAT a large sauté pan over medium-high heat. Add oil to pan, swirl to coat. Add asparagus and cook 1 minute. Sprinkle evenly with grated lemon rind, ground black pepper and salt. Toss to coat. Sprinkle with cheese.

Parmesan Rosemary Polenta

SERVES 4 TO 6

- 3 cups water
- ¾ cup instant polenta (or regular polenta)
- 4 tbsp Parmesan cheese, grated
- 1 tsp fresh rosemary, minced
- ¼ tsp sea salt
- 2 tbsp unsalted grass-fed butter

COOK polenta according to package directions.

STIR in cheese, rosemary, butter and salt. Serve immediately.

Savory Black Beans

SERVES 6

- 1 pound dried black beans
- 4 cups low-sodium chicken broth
- 3 garlic cloves, minced
- 1 medium yellow or red onion, peeled and diced
- 1 red bell pepper, seeded and diced
- 1 green bell pepper, seeded and diced
- 1 yellow bell pepper, seeded and diced
- 1½ tsp ground chili powder + more if needed
- 1½ tsp ground cumin + more in needed
- 1 tsp sea salt + more to taste
- – fresh cilantro leaves, lime wedges and diced bell peppers for serving

PLACE the beans in a bowl or pot, cover with cold water and allow to soak overnight. Drain and rinse before proceeding. (Alternatively, add the beans to a medium pot and cover with hot water. Bring to a boil, and then boil for 2 minutes. Turn off the heat, cover the pot and allow the beans to sit for 1 hour. Drain the beans and rinse them with cold water before proceeding.)

ADD the soaked beans, chicken broth, 2 cups water, the garlic, onions and green, red and yellow bell peppers to a stockpot. Bring to a boil, reduce the heat to low, cover and simmer for 90 minutes. Add the chili powder, cumin and salt and stir. Cover and continue simmering until the liquid level is to your liking, about another hour. Taste for seasoning and add more of whatever it needs.

TIP! Save the leftover polenta and put it into a baking pan to set in the refrigerator. Remove from pan and cut into 1-inch squares. Bake at 400 for about an hour on a parchment-paper lined baking sheet until crispy for the best croutons ever.

Green Bean & Garlic Sauté

SERVES 4

- 2 cups green beans, ends trimmed
- 1 tbsp unsalted grass-fed butter
- ¼ cup almonds, slivered or sliced
- – sea salt and freshly ground black pepper to taste

SAUTÉ the green beans in butter until tender-crisp in a sauté pan. Season with salt and black pepper to taste. Before serving, add the almonds to the pan and heat through until the almonds are toasted.

Broccolini Sauté

SERVES 2

- 1 bunch broccolini, ends trimmed
- 2 tbsp unsalted, grass-fed butter
- – zest of ½ lemon
- 1 tsp garlic, minced
- ¼ tbsp lemon juice
- ¼ tsp sea salt
- ¼ tsp freshly ground black pepper

BLANCH the broccolini in a large pot of boiling salted water for 2 minutes. Drain immediately and immerse in a bowl of ice water.

MELT butter in a large sauté pan. Add the lemon zest and garlic and stir. Drain the broccolini and add it to the garlic mixture and heat for 2 minutes. Add the lemon juice, salt and the pepper, and toss well before serving.

Roasted Broccolini with Winey Mushrooms

SERVES 4

- 3 large bunches broccolini, ends trimmed
- 4 tbsp olive or avocado oil
- 1 tsp sea salt
- 1 small sweet onion, finely diced
- 2 cups cremini mushrooms, thinly sliced
- ¼ cup dry white wine
- ¼ tsp freshly ground black pepper
- – Parmesan cheese, grated

PREHEAT oven to 400 degrees. On a baking sheet, drizzle broccolini with 2 tbsp oil; sprinkle with ½ tsp salt and toss to coat. Spread in a single layer. Roast, turning once with tongs until crisp-tender, about 10 to 15 minutes. If stems are not uniform in size, remove thinner ones to a platter once done. (Broccolini can be cooked hours in advance and kept at room temp).

HEAT remaining oil over medium heat in a large, deep sauté pan. Add onion and cook, stirring occasionally, until it starts to soften, about 5 minutes. Raise heat to medium high, add mushrooms and remaining salt and cook, stirring occasionally, until mushrooms are golden brown, 7 to 10 minutes. Mushrooms will release liquid before reabsorbing it and browning. Add wine, cook until pan is dry, about 2 minutes. Stir in pepper.

SPOON mushrooms over broccolini. Scatter some Parmesan over dish, if desired. Serve warm or at room temperature.

NUTRITION FACTS

PER SERVING: 241 CALORIES, 14G FAT (2G SATURATED), 0MG CHOLESTEROL, 3G FIBER, 8G PROTEIN, 21G CARBS, 540MG SODIUM, 148MG CALCIUM

Salads

Friends are the bacon bits in the salad bowl of life.

Making one simple change to your diet—adding a salad almost every day—is one of the most healthy eating habits you can adopt. And one of the simplest. It's a convenient way to get more veggies, greens and fruit in each day to hit your 6 to 10 servings per day goal. Plus, salads are full of textures and flavors that excite the palate.

Heirloom Tomato Salad

SERVES 2

1	pound heirloom tomatoes (mix up the colors for a variety of tastes and a more interesting salad)
½	cup bocconcini (baby mozzarella)
1	generous handful basil leaves
8	sprigs of fresh chives
⅛	cup high-quality balsamic vinegar
⅛	cup extra-virgin olive oil
½	tsp sea salt
–	freshly ground black pepper to taste

WASH the tomatoes well. Slice them into ¼-inch or ½-inch slices and divide the tomatoes between two plates.

BREAK up the bocconcini and divide the pieces among the plates. Drop whole basil leaves on top of the tomatoes and cheese.

DISTRIBUTE the chives by snipping with scissors and letting pieces fall over salad. Drizzle ½ tbsp balsamic vinegar over each salad followed by 1 tbsp oil, and dust with salt and pepper.

NUTRITIONAL FACTS

PER SERVING: 240 CALORIES, 7G PROTEIN, 8G CARBS, 20G FAT (PRIMARILY FROM THE EXTRA-VIRGIN OLIVE OIL), 1.5G FIBER, 578MG SODIUM, 6G SUGAR

TIP! Balsamic vinegar is a lot like wine—the older the better. Try to purchase the best quality vinegar you can. It makes a big difference in the taste.

Lentil Salad

SERVES 2

- 1 tsp Dijon mustard
- 1 tbsp red wine or sherry vinegar
- 2 tbsp extra-virgin olive oil
- ½ tsp sea salt + more to taste
- – freshly ground black pepper to taste
- 2 cups lentils (brown, green or red)
- 1 large ripe tomato, chopped
- ½ large cucumber, peeled, seeded and chopped
- ½ cup carrots, peeled and chopped
- ½ cup red bell pepper, seeded and chopped
- 3 tbsp red onion, chopped
- 2 tsp fresh cilantro, chopped

PREPARE lentils according to package directions. Drain and set aside.

MIX mustard, vinegar, oil, salt and pepper in a large bowl with 1 tbsp water, whisk until well combined

ADD remaining ingredients to bowl and toss until coated with dressing. Season to taste.

Sicilian Farro & Tuna Salad

SERVES 2

- 2 ½ cups water
- ¾ cup semi-pearled farro
- 1 can water-packed tuna, drained
- ¼ cup golden raisins
- 6 pitted green olives, chopped
- 2 tbsp capers, drained and chopped
- 2 ½ tbsp freshly squeezed lemon juice
- 1 tbsp Dijon mustard
- 2 tbsp extra-virgin olive oil
- 4 cups baby arugula
- – sea salt and freshly ground pepper to taste

BRING water to a boil in a large saucepan. Add farro and simmer, partially covered, over medium-low heat 30 minutes. Turn off heat, cover pot and let farro rest 5 minutes. Fluff with a fork and transfer to a large serving bowl to cool, about 10 minutes.

ADD tuna, raisins, olives and capers; stir well to break up tuna. Stir in lemon juice, mustard and oil. Add arugula and gently toss to combine; season with salt and pepper to taste.

Mexican Quinoa Salad

SERVES 4

- 3 cups baby arugula
- 1 15-ounce can unsalted black beans, rinsed and drained
- 1 large jeweled sweet potato, peeled and cubed
- ½ cup cucumber, sliced
- ½ cup bell pepper, seeded and chopped
- 1 cup cherry or Roma tomatoes, chopped
- 1 avocado, pitted and diced
- 3 tbsp grated pepper jack cheese
- ½ tsp each cumin, cinnamon and sea salt, divided
- 1 cup dry white or red quinoa
- – olive oil or coconut oil

PREHEAT oven to 400 degrees and prep sweet potatoes. Toss with a drizzle of olive oil and ¼ tsp each cumin, cinnamon and sea salt. Bake for 20 to 25 minutes or until tender and slightly golden brown.

RINSE quinoa in a fine mesh strainer and place in a small saucepan over medium-high heat to toast. Stir and cook for 2 to 3 minutes and then add 1½ cups water and stir. Bring to a boil, then reduce heat to simmer, cover and cook for 15 minutes or until tender and the water is fully absorbed. Turn off heat and set aside.

BRING black beans to a simmer over medium heat in a separate saucepan, and season with ¼ tsp each sea salt, cumin and cinnamon. Once bubbly and warm, turn heat to simmer/low.

CHOP vegetables and tomatoes and set aside.

PREPARE dressing using the *Cilantro Lime Dressing* recipe (see *Condiments & Dressings* section).

ASSEMBLE salad with all ingredients into two bowls. Drizzle with dressing and toss to lightly coat. Serve with ¼ tsp chopped fresh cilantro on top.

Simple Avocado Quinoa Salad

SERVES 4

- 2 cups red or white quinoa, cooked and drained
- ¼ cup red onion, thinly sliced
- 1 Fuji apple, thinly sliced into half moons
- 2 cups Lacinato or green curly kale leaves, chopped into ribbons
- – juice of 1 lemon
- 2 tbsp extra-vigin olive oil
- 2 tsp organic honey
- 1 pinch sea salt
- 1 ripe avocado, pitted and cubed
- 10 cherry tomatoes, halved

TOSS quinoa, onions, apple and kale in a large salad bowl to combine.

DRIZZLE in lemon juice, oil, honey, and salt, and toss to coat well.

FOLD in avocado and tomatoes gently. Serve chilled or at room temperature.

NUTRITION FACTS

PER SERVING: 293 CALORIES, 16G FAT (2G SATURATED), 35G CARBS, 6G PROTEIN, 7G FIBER, 72MG CALCIUM, 97MG SODIUM

Israeli Salad

SERVES 4

- 2 extra-large tomatoes
- 1 cucumber
- ½ medium red onion
- 1 red bell pepper
- — juice from ¼ lemon + more to taste
- — zest of 1 lemon
- 4 tbsp extra-virgin olive oil
- — sea salt and freshly ground black pepper to taste
- ¼ cup chopped herbs (flat-leaf parsley, mint, cilantro)

CHOP the first four ingredients into a small dice.

PLACE them in a large bowl and toss with the fresh herbs, lemon zest, olive oil, lemon juice, salt and pepper.

Greek Vegetable Salad

SERVES 4

- 1 cup tomatoes, chopped
- ½ cup cucumber, chopped
- ¼ cup bell pepper, chopped
- 2 tbsp red onion, chopped
- ¾ tsp snipped fresh thyme or ¼ tsp dried thyme, crushed
- ½ tsp snipped fresh oregano or ¼ tsp dried oregano, crushed
- 1 white or regular balsamic vinegar
- 1 tbsp extra-virgin olive oil
- ¼ cup crumbled reduced-fat feta cheese

COMBINE tomatoes, cucumber, bell pepper, red onion and herbs in a medium bowl.

WHISK together olive oil and vinegar in a small bowl.

POUR dressing over vegetable mixture. Toss gently to coat. Sprinkle with cheese before serving.

NUTRITION FACTS

PER SERVING (½ CUP): 65 CALORIES, 5G FAT, 3MG CHOLESTEROL, 120MG SODIUM, 4G CARBS, 1G FIBER, 2G PROTEIN

Summer Panzelella Salad

SERVES 2

- 3 tbsp extra-virgin olive oil
- 1 small French bread or sourdough, cut into 1-inch cubes (about 6 cups)
- 1 tsp sea salt
- 15 ripe cherry tomatoes, halved
- 1 cucumber, unpeeled, seeded and sliced ½-inch thick
- 2 bell peppers, seeded, cut into 1-inch cubes (use a combination of colors)
- ½ red onion, thinly sliced
- 20 large basil leaves, coarsely chopped

HEAT the oil in a large sauté pan. Add the bread and salt; cook over low to medium heat, tossing frequently, for 10 minutes, or until nicely browned. Add more oil as needed.

PREPARE the *Simple Vinaigrette* (see *Condiments & Dressings* section).

MIX the tomatoes, cucumber, peppers, red onion and basil in a large bowl. Add the bread cubes and toss with the vinaigrette. Season liberally with salt and pepper.

SERVE immediately if needed, or allow the salad to sit for about 30 minutes for the flavors to blend.

Kale & Stonefruit Salad

SERVES 2

- 10 stalks green curly or Lacinato kale
- 3 tbsp extra-virgin olive oil
- 1 tbsp fresh lime juice
- 1 cup red cabbage, shredded
- 1 cup green cabbage or Brussels sprouts, shredded
- 1 medium stone fruit (peach or nectarine), sliced into thin pieces
- 1 small handfull fresh cilantro. chopped
- 1 large handful fresh flat-leaf parsley, chopped
- ¼ cup red onion, diced

Dressing
- 2 tbsp fresh lime juice
- 2 tbsp extra-virgin olive oil
- 1 tbsp apple cider vinegar
- – zest from 1 lime
- 1 tsp sea salt
- – heavy pinch of black pepper

COMBINE all dressing ingredients in a small bowl and whisk for about 15 seconds. Set aside.

WASH, dry and remove ribs from kale and cut the kale into finely shredded pieces. Toss the kale in a large bowl with olive oil, lime juice and sea salt. Massage it with your hands for 3 minutes to allow the kale to soak up the liquid.

ADD the cabbage (and/or Brussels sprouts), stone fruit, cilantro, parsley and red onion. Combine well. Drizzle on the dressing and serve.

Kale, Carrot & Avocado Salad

SERVES 2

- ½ bunch green curly kale, de-stemmed and chopped into ribbons
- ½ cup carrot, peeled and grated
- ½ ripe avocado, peeled and pitted
- ¼ cup red onion, thinly sliced
- 1 tbsp lemon or lime juice
- 1 tbsp pumpkin seeds, toasted
- ¼ tsp reduced sodium soy sauce or Bragg's Liquid Aminos

TOAST pumpkin seeds in sauté pan over medium-high heat for a few minutes; set aside.

TOSS all ingredients together in a large bowl. Use your hands to thoroughly mash avocado into kale. Set aside at room temperature for 30 minutes before serving to allow kale to soften.

NUTRITION FACTS
PER SERVING: 160 CALORIES, 7G TOTAL FAT, 0MG CHOLESTEROL, 115MG SODIUM, 23G CARBS, 6G FIBER, 3G SUGAR, 6G PROTEIN

Kale, Grains & Blueberry Salad

SERVES 8

- 1 cup wheat berries
- 1 tsp sea salt
- 1 8-ounce package sugar snap peas
- 4 cups green curly kale, coarsely chopped
- ½ cup *Red Wine Vinaigrette* (see *Condiments & Dressings* section)
- 2 cups fresh blueberries
- ½ cup pecans, toasted and roughly chopped
- ¾ cup crumbled feta cheese

BRING wheat berries, salt and 4 cups water to a boil in a saucepan. Cover, reduce heat to low, and simmer 1 hour.

BLANCH peas in boiling salted water for 2 minutes or until crisp-tender. Drain and plunge into ice water to stop the cooking (shock). Drain and pat dry. Slice in half. Drain wheat berries; rinse under cold water until cool.

TOSS together kale, wheat berries, and ¼ cup vinaigrette in a large bowl. Let stand 30 minutes. Stir in blueberries, pecans, and sugar snap peas. Add salt and pepper. Sprinkle with cheese (leave off feta if you are not eating dairy--the salad will still taste great). Serve with remaining vinaigrette.

Apple, Carrot & Cabbage Chopped Salad

SERVES 6

- 2½ tbsp extra-virgin olive oil
- 1 tbsp juice from an orange
- 2 tsp white wine vinegar
- ½ tsp ground cumin
- ¼ tsp ground cinnamon
- 3 cups carrots, peeled and shredded
- 1 cup red cabbage, chopped
- 1 large red or green apple, cored and chopped
- 1 cup sunflower sprouts (sub micro arugula if desired, or leave out if you can't find either)
- ½ cup fresh cilantro leaves
- 3 tbsp sunflower or pumpkin seeds, lightly toasted
- – freshly ground black pepper to taste
- – lime wedges for serving

TOAST seeds in sauté pan over medium-high heat for a few minutes. Set aside.

WHISK oil, orange juice, vinegar, salt, cinnamon and cumin in a large bowl. Add carrots, cabbage, apple, sunflower sprouts, cilantro, and sunflower seeds.

TOSS to combine with the dressing. Season with pepper. Serve with lime wedges if desired.

NUTRITION FACTS

PER SERVING (1⅓ CUP): 124 CALORIES, 8G FAT, 0MG CHOLESTEROL, 13G CARBS, 6G SUGARS, 2G PROTEIN, 3G FIBER, 137MG SODIUM

Southwestern Chopped Salad

SERVES 2

- 5 cups chopped romaine lettuce, rinsed and patted dry
- ½ cup cherry tomatoes, halved
- ½ cup corn kernels (fresh, thawed or canned), drained
- ½ cup canned black beans, drained and rinsed
- 2 tbsp fresh cilantro, chopped
- 1 ripe avocado, pitted and diced
- ¼ cup crumbled tortilla chips
- ¼ cup *Cilantro Lime Dressing* (see *Condiments & Dressings* section)

PREP the dressing and set aside.

ASSEMBLE the salad by placing romaine lettuce in a large bowl; top with tomatoes, corn, black beans and cilantro. Pour the dressing on top of the salad and gently toss to combine. Stir in avocado.

SERVE immediately, garnished with tortillas chips, if desired.

Roasted Vegetable & Farro Salad

SERVES 4 TO 6

1	cup dry semi-pearled farro
1½	cups water
4	medium carrots, scrubbed and cut into ½-inch slices
1	cup Brussels sprouts, trimmed and quartered
¼	cup + 1 tbsp extra-virgin olive oil
½	tsp sea salt
2	cups lightly packed green curly kale leaves, thinly sliced
4	large dried Mission figs, stemmed and chopped
1	tbsp za'atar spice blend
¼	cup red wine vinegar
1	tsp organic honey
¼	cup crumbled feta cheese
3	tbsp chopped almonds

COMBINE the farro and water in a medium saucepan over medium-high heat. Bring the water to a boil, then reduce the heat so the liquid is barely bubbling; cover and cook for 20 minutes. Remove from the heat; drain any excess water, cover and let stand for at least 10 minutes or until it cools to room temp.

PREHEAT oven to 500 degrees.

TOSS the carrots and Brussels sprouts on a rimmed baking sheet with 1 tbsp of the oil and the salt. Roast until the Brussels sprouts are caramelized around the edges and the carrots are barely tender (but not soft) when pierced with a fork, 10 to 15 minutes. Let cool to room temperature

PLACE kale in a serving bowl and massage the leaves by picking them up by the handful and squeezing/crumpling them. Repeat for a few minutes, until the kale turns silky and darkens in color. Add the figs, almonds, cooked farro and roasted carrots and Brussels sprouts; toss to combine.

WHISK together the remaining ¼ cup of oil, the za'atar, vinegar and honey in a medium bowl to form an emulsified vinaigrette, then stir in the feta. Pour over the salad and toss to incorporate.

Arugula & Raddicchio Pizza Salad

SERVES 4

1	tbsp red wine vinegar
½	tsp sugar
¼	tsp sea salt
1	garlic clove, minced
1	tbsp extra-virgin olive oil
2	cups baby arugula
1	cup sliced radicchio
–	all purpose flour and cornmeal
1	pound whole wheat (or gluten-free) pizza dough, room temperature
½	cup fontina cheese, grated
½	cup red onion, sliced
2	tbsp Parmesan cheese shavings

PLACE oven rack on lowest position and preheat to 500 degrees.

ROLL dough into a 14-inch round on a lightly floured surface. Generously sprinkle a baking sheet with cornmeal. Place dough on sheet. Top with Fontina, leaving a ½-inch border.

BAKE until cheese has melted and crust is crisp, about 13 minutes.

WHISK vinegar, sugar, salt, garlic and oil together in a large bowl. Toss in arugula, radicchio and onion; spread on pizza. Top with Parmesan. Cut into 8 slices. Serve immediately.

Soups, Stews & Chilis

Happiness is ... homemade soup

Who doesn't love a warm bowl of soup? Soup, chili and stew are one-pot wonders that make really nutritious meals and they make food prep and planning so much easier since you'll have extras to eat another time.

Making soups and chili is a regular part of my food prep process, and it always serves me well. Especially when I'm having one of those "what can I eat" moments and I don't feel like cooking. Open the freezer, defrost, warm up and voila ... a healthy meal in just a few minutes!

Chicken Tortilla Soup

SERVES 6

2½	tbsp avocado or coconut oil
½	medium red or white onion, diced
3	carrots, peeled and roughly chopped
3	medium celery stalks, roughly chopped
2	medium red or yellow bell peppers, roughly chopped
4	garlic cloves, minced
½	tsp chili powder
1	tbsp ground coriander
2	tbsp ground cumin
1	tsp dried oregano
¼	to ½ tsp ground paprika
¼	ground cayenne pepper (leave out if you don't like spicy)
1	carton low-sodium chicken or vegetable stock
1	to 2 cups water
1	15-ounce can fire-roasted diced tomatoes
1½	tsp sea salt + more to taste
½	tsp freshly ground black pepper + more to taste
4	6-inch corn tortillas, cut into ½-inch pieces
2	15-ounce cans black beans, rinsed and trained
2	cups chicken, cooked and shredded (use a whole roasted one from the store to lessen prep time)
–	juice of 1 lime

HEAT the oil in a large stockpot or Dutch oven over medium heat until shimmering. Add the onion, carrot, celery, and bell pepper and season with salt and pepper. Cook, stirring occasionally, until the vegetables have softened, about 6 minutes.

ADD the garlic, chili powder, coriander, cumin, oregano, paprika, and cayenne. Cook, stirring occasionally until fragrant, about 2 minutes. Stir in broth, water, tomatoes, salt and pepper, and bring to a boil.

REDUCE the heat to low, add the tortillas and stir to combine. Simmer, stirring occasionally, until the tortillas have disintegrated and the soup has thickened, about 1 hour.

ADD chicken and black beans and stir. Simmer for 15 to 20 minutes until the flavors meld. Taste and season with salt and pepper as needed.

SERVE with preferred toppings such as avocado slices and chopped cilantro.

Classic Chicken & Vegetable Soup

SERVES 6

- 1½ tbsp avocado or coconut oil
- 1 medium white onion, diced
- 3 large carrots, peeled and roughly chopped
- 5 celery stalks, roughly chopped
- 3 garlic cloves, minced
- 4 sprigs fresh thyme, destemmed and chopped (or 1 tbsp dried thyme)
- 1 roasted chicken, shredded (or 1 pound organic boneless and skinless breasts, cut into 1-inch chunks)
- 1 carton low-sodium chicken or vegetable stock + water if needed to cover veggies and chicken
- 1½ tsp sea salt + more to taste
- — freshly ground black pepper to taste

MELT cooking fat in a large stockpot or Dutch oven over medium heat and gently sauté the onion, garlic and chicken (if not using store-bought roasted chicken) for about 5 minutes, until the onion is tender.

ADD the carrots, celery, thyme and enough broth to cover the vegetables. Bring soup to a boil, then reduce heat and allow to simmer for 20 minutes. If using store-bought chicken, add in now and allow to heat up for 10 to 15 minutes.

SEASON with salt and pepper to taste.

Chicken & Wild Rice Soup

SERVES 6

- 2 tbsp avocado or coconut oil
- 1 medium white onion, diced
- 3 large carrots, peeled and roughly chopped
- 5 celery stalks, roughly chopped
- 3 garlic cloves, minced
- 4 sprigs fresh thyme, destemmed and chopped (or 1 tbsp dried thyme)
- 1 roasted chicken, shredded (or 1 pound organic boneless and skinless breasts, cut into 1-inch chunks)
- 1 carton low-sodium chicken or vegetable stock + water if needed to cover veggies and chicken
- 1 cup wild rice
- 1½ tsp sea salt + more to taste
- — freshly ground black pepper to taste

MELT cooking fat in large stockpot or Dutch oven over medium heat and gently sauté the onion, garlic and chicken (if not using store-bought roasted chicken) for about 5 minutes, until the onion is tender.

ADD carrots, celery, thyme, rice and enough broth to cover the vegetables. Bring the soup to a boil, then reduce heat and allow to simmer for 20 minutes. If using store-bought chicken, add in now, and allow the soup to warm up for about 10 to 15 minutes.

SEASON with salt and pepper to taste.

White Bean & Kale Soup

SERVES 4

- 2 tbsp avocado or coconut oil
- 1 cup yellow onion, diced
- 4 garlic cloves, minced
- 2 large carrots, peeled and thinly sliced
- 1 carton low-sodium vegetable broth
- 4 cups green curly kale, de-stemmed and thinly sliced
- 1 15-ounce can fire-roasted diced tomatoes
- 1 15-ounce can unsalted cannellini beans, drained and rinsed

MELT cooking fat in a stockpot over medium heat. Add onion and cook 3 minutes. Add garlic and cook 2 minutes longer.

ADD broth, kale, carrots and tomatoes and cover. Cook 5 minutes or until kale is tender.

ADD beans and heat thoroughly.

NUTRITION FACTS

PER SERVING (1 CUP): 284 CALORIES, 8G FAT, 0MG CHOLESTEROL, 460MG SODIUM, 33G CARBS, 8G FIBER, 7G SUGAR, 9G PROTEIN

Spicy Shrimp, Farro & Greens Soup

SERVES 5 TO 6

- 2 tbsp avocado or coconut oil
- 4 large shallots, peeled and coarsely chopped
- 2 large carrots, peeled and roughly chopped
- ¼ to ½ tsp red chili pepper flakes (adjust to your preferred level of heat)
- 4 garlic cloves, minced
- – sea salt and freshly ground black pepper
- 1 15-ounce can fire-roasted diced tomatoes
- 8 cups low-sodium chicken broth
- 1 cup dry semi-pearled farro
- 1 pound raw shrimp, peeled and deveined
- 8 cups Swiss chard or green curly kale, de-stemmed and torn
- – torn basil leaves and crusty bread for serving

HEAT oil in a stockpot or Dutch oven over medium-high heat. Add the shallots, carrot, chili pepper flakes, garlic, and ¼ teaspoon each salt and pepper and cook, stirring often, until the vegetables are just tender, 6 to 8 minutes. Add the tomatoes and broth and bring to a boil. Add the farro and cook until tender, 20 to 25 minutes.

STIR in the shrimp and chard and cook until the shrimp are opaque, 2 to 4 minutes. Transfer the soup to bowls and sprinkle with the basil. Serve with the bread.

Black Bean Soup

SERVES 6 TO 8

2	tbsp avocado or coconut oil
1	medium white or red onion, diced
3	ribs celery, rough chopped
3	large carrots, diced
2	bell peppers (any color), diced
4	garlic cloves, minced
1	15-ounce can fire-roasted diced tomatoes
5	15-ounce cans low-sodium organic black beans, rinsed and drained
–	juice of 1 lime
1	tsp sea salt
1	tbsp + 1 tsp ground cumin
1	tbsp dried oregano
½	tsp chili powder
⅛	tsp red chili pepper flakes
1	carton low-sodium vegetable broth + water if needed to completely cover veggies and beans
–	freshly ground black pepper to taste
¼	cup fresh cilantro

Toppings
Cilantro, red onion, guacamole, avocado slices, pico de gallo

HEAT oil in stockpot over medium heat. Add onion, celery, carrot, pepper and garlic. Sauté until tender, about 7 minutes.

ADD beans, salt, cumin, oregano, chili powder, chili pepper flakes and diced tomatoes, stirring until combined. Heat through, about 5 minutes. If ingredients start to stick to pot, add ¼ cup broth.

ADD vegetable broth (and water if needed) until it covers the veggie and beans mixture. Allow soup to come to a boil, then turn heat down to medium low and simmer 15 minutes. Toss in cilantro, add lime juice and stir.

BLEND the soup until smooth with immersion blender.

ADD your choice of toppings and serve immediately.

Soups, Stews & Chilis

Roasted Butternut Squash Soup

SERVES 6

- 2 tbsp avocado or coconut oil
- 1 medium white onion, roughly chopped
- 2 Honeycrisp or Fuji apples, cored and chopped
- 2 medium carrots, peeled and cut into ½-inch pieces
- 5 garlic cloves
- 7 cups butternut squash, peeled, seeded and cut into ¾-inch chunks (buy this pre-done from the store to save time)
- ½ cup fresh sage, chopped
- 1 carton low-sodium chicken or vegetable stock + more water to cover veggies
- – sea salt and freshly ground black pepper to taste

HEAT oven to 400 degrees. Place squash, onion, carrot and apples on 2 baking sheets and drizzle with oil. Salt and pepper to taste. Cut ends off of garlic cloves and drizzle with oil. Wrap in a little foil. Roast for 35 minutes in the oven, or until you see good charring. Remove pans from oven.

PLACE all cooked veggies in a large stockpot or Dutch oven and add broth plus enough water to cover veggie mixture. Add chopped sage. Heat to a boil, then reduce heat to medium, cooking for 10 minutes.

TAKE pot off heat and blend soup with immersion blender until smooth. Add more water until you reach desired consistency if needed. Salt and pepper to taste.

NUTRITION FACTS

PER SERVING (1¼ CUPS SOUP): 127 CALORIES, 4G FAT, 29G CARBS, 8G PROTEIN, 6G FIBER, 182MG CALCIUM, 2MG IRON, 248MG SODIUM

Roasted Tomato Soup

SERVES 6

- 6 pounds tomatoes, halved
- – cooking spray
- – sea salt and freshly ground black pepper to taste
- 2 medium yellow onions, diced
- 6 garlic cloves, minced
- ¼ tsp crushed red pepper or red chili pepper flakes
- 2 tbsp extra-virgin olive oil
- 4 cups basil leaves, chopped
- 3 to 4 cups water
- 2 tbsp balsamic vinegar

PREHEAT oven to 400 degrees. Mist tomatoes with cooking spray, arrange on baking sheet skin-side-down, and sprinkle with salt and pepper to taste. Roast for 45 minutes, then set aside.

SAUTÉ onions, garlic and crushed red pepper with oil in large stockpot or Dutch oven over medium-high heat for five minutes. Salt and pepper to taste. Add roasted tomatoes, basil, water and more salt and pepper to taste, if desired. Pureé mixture with immersion blender until semi-smooth. Bring to a boil, cover, and simmer for 15 minutes.

SERVE soup with a drizzle of balsamic vinegar on top.

NUTRITION FACTS

PER SERVING (1 CUP): 140 CALORIES, 18G CARBS, 2G FAT, 3G PROTEIN

TIP! Word to the wise when making blended soup recipes … get yourself a hand-held immersion blender and save the rush trip to the ER to treat the burns you'll get from trying to transfer hot soup from the pot to a traditional blender.

Cauliflower & Smoked Gouda Soup

SERVES 6

- 2 tsp avocado oil
- ¾ tsp ground white pepper, divided
- 1 tbsp fresh thyme, de-stemmed and chopped
- ¼ tsp garlic powder
- 1 large sweet onion, chopped
- ¼ tsp sea salt
- 2 tsp smoked paprika
- ¼ cup dry white wine
- 1 large head cauliflower, cored and chopped
- 1 carton low-sodium chicken or vegetable broth, divided
- 2 tsp cornstarch
- ¾ cup shredded smoked Gouda
- ¼ cup heavy cream

HEAT 2 tsp oil in a large stockpot or Dutch oven over medium heat. Add onion and salt, cover and cook, stirring occasionally, until the onion is very soft and barely starting to brown, 7 to 9 minutes. Sprinkle with paprika, white pepper and thyme. Cook, stirring, until fragrant, 30 seconds to 1 minute. Add wine, increase heat to high and bring to a boil, scraping up any browned bits.

ADD cauliflower and 3½ cups broth, cover and bring to a boil, stirring often. Reduce heat to maintain a simmer and cook until the cauliflower is very tender, 10 to 12 minutes.

PUREÉ the soup in the pot with an immersion blender. Combine the remaining ½ cup broth and cornstarch in a small bowl and stir into the soup. Return to a simmer over medium heat; simmer, stirring constantly, for 1 minute. Remove from heat. Stir in cheese and cream until fully incorporated. Serve immediately.

Creamy Asparagus Potato Soup

SERVES 6

- 1½ tbsp avocado or coconut oil
- 4 medium shallots, peeled and diced
- ½ medium white onion, diced
- 3 garlic cloves, minced
- 2 bunches asparagus, woody ends removed and cut into 1-inch pieces
- 2½ cups small red or gold potatoes, halved or quartered
- 1½ carton low-sodium chicken or vegetable stock (+ more if needed to cover veggies)
- ½ tsp sea salt
- ½ tsp freshly ground black pepper
- 1 tsp dried thyme

Optional Topping
- 1 cup whole grain bread in ¼-inch cubes
- — scallion greens, sliced

HEAT 1 tbsp oil in a large stockpot or Dutch oven over medium heat. Add shallot, onion and garlic and cook, stirring, until softened, 2 to 3 minutes. Add broth, asparagus, potatoes, salt and pepper; bring to a boil. Reduce heat and simmer until the veggies are tender, about 15 minutes. Pureé with immersion blender until smooth. Salt and pepper to taste.

HEAT the remaining 1½ tablespoons oil in a large sauté pan over medium-high heat. Reduce heat to medium, add bread cubes and cook, stirring, until browned and crispy, 3 to 5 minutes. Serve the soup topped with the croutons and scallions, if desired.

NUTRITION FACTS

PER SERVING (1 CUP + 2 CROUTONS): 190 CALORIES, 10G FAT, 22G CARBS, 0MG CHOLESTEROL, 4G SUGAR, 5G PROTEIN; 5G FIBER, 338MG SODIUM, 428MG POTASSIUM

Creamy Broccoli Soup

SERVES 6

1	tbsp avocado or coconut oil
1	medium white onion, diced
2	garlic cloves, minced
2	pounds broccoli stems and crowns, roughly chopped
¼	tsp sea salt
1	pinch freshly ground black pepper
1	carton low-sodium vegetable broth
¼	cup fresh lemon juice
–	small blanched broccoli florets for garnish

HEAT oil in large stockpot or Dutch oven over medium heat. Add onion and garlic and cook until softened, about 7 minutes. Add broccoli, salt and pepper; stir well to coat. Add broth and lemon juice, and bring to a simmer.

PARTIALLY COVER, reduce heat to low, and simmer gently until broccoli is very tender, about 25 minutes. Use immersion blender to pureé soup. Serve hot, garnished with a small broccoli floret, if desired.

NUTRITION FACTS

PER SERVING (1 CUP): 80 CALORIES, 390MG SODIUM, 12G CARBS, 4G FIBER, 2.5G FAT, 4G PROTEIN

Winter Minestrone

SERVES 6

- 2 tbsp avocado or coconut oil
- 1 medium white onion, diced
- 3 small carrots, peeled and diced
- 3 celery stalks, diced
- 3 ounces thinly sliced pancetta, coarsely chopped
- 3 garlic cloves, minced
- 1 bunch Swiss chard, de-stemmed, coarsely chopped
- 1 jeweled sweet potato, peeled and cubed
- 1 15-ounce can fire-roasted diced tomatoes
- 1 15-ounce can unsalted cannellini beans
- 1 sprig fresh rosemary
- 1 carton low-sodium chicken or vegetable stock
- 1 ounce piece Parmesan cheese + rind
- 2 tbsp flat-leaf parsely, chopped
- – sea salt and freshly ground black pepper to taste

HEAT oil in a large stockpot or Dutch oven over medium heat. Add the onion, carrots, celery, pancetta, and garlic. Sauté until the onion is translucent, about 8 to 10 minutes. Add the Swiss chard and potato; sauté for 2 minutes. Add the tomatoes and rosemary sprig. Simmer until the chard is wilted and the tomatoes break down, about 10 minutes.

BLEND ¾ cup of the beans with ¼ cup of the broth in a processor until almost smooth. Add the pureéd bean mixture, remaining broth, and Parmesan cheese rind to the vegetable mixture. Simmer until the potato pieces are tender, stirring occasionally, about 15 minutes. Stir in the whole beans and parsley.

SIMMER until the beans are heated through and the soup is thick, about 2 minutes. Season to taste with salt and pepper.

SEARCH the soup pot for the Parmesan rind and rosemary sprig (the leaves will have fallen off the stem) and discard these. Garnish with a small amount of freshly grated Parmesan cheese and serve.

NUTRITION FACTS

PER SERVING (1 CUP): 375 CALORIES, 15G FAT, 19G PROTEIN, 43G CARBS, 10G SUGAR, 10G FIBER, 1,391MG SODIUM

(Lower the sodium by using low-sodium versions of all canned ingredients and broth, and consider skipping the pancetta).

Hungarian Beef Stew

SERVES 4

- 1¼ pound lean boneless chuck roast, trimmed and cut into 1-inch chunks
- ¾ tsp sea salt, divided
- ½ tsp freshly ground black pepper
- 2 tbsps coconut or avocado oil
- 2 medium white onions, chopped
- 3 medium carrots, peeled and coarsely chopped
- 2 red bell peppers, coarsely chopped
- 2 tbsp gluten-free or all-purpose flour
- 3 garlic cloves, minced
- 1 cup small gold/red or fingerling potatoes, chopped
- 2 cups water, divided
- 1½ cups low-sodium beef stock or broth
- 1 cup dry red wine
- 1 tsp smoked paprika
- 1 tsp caraway seeds
- — sea salt and freshly ground black pepper to taste

SPRINKLE beef with ½ teaspoon salt and ¼ tsp pepper. Heat oil in a large Dutch oven or stockpot over medium-high heat. Add ⅓ of beef to pan; cook 6 minutes or until golden brown on both sides. Transfer to a plate. Repeat procedure with remaining beef in 2 more batches.

REDUCE heat to medium, and add onions to pan; cook 5 minutes or until softened. Add flour, paprika, caraway seeds, and garlic; cook 1 minute, stirring. Add wine; cook 2 minutes or until thickened, stirring occasionally and scraping browned bits from bottom of pan.

ADD 1 cup water, stock, and beef to pan; bring to a simmer. Reduce heat to low; cook for 1¼ hours. Stir in potatoes, carrots, peppers, and remaining 1 cup water; simmer, partially covered, for 45 minutes to an hour or until meat and vegetables are fork-tender. Season stew with remaining ¼ teaspoon salt and ¼ teaspoon pepper.

White Turkey Chili

SERVES 6

- 3 tbsp avocado or coconut oil
- 1 pound lean ground turkey
- 1 large white onion, diced
- 4 garlic cloves, minced
- 2 medium zucchini, diced
- ½ cup dry red or white quinoa
- 2 tbsp dried oregano
- 3 tsp ground cumin
- ½ tsp ground coriander
- ½ tsp freshly ground black pepper
- ¼ tsp sea salt
- 2 15-ounce cans low-sodium cannellini beans, rinsed
- 2 4-ounce cans green chilies
- 1 carton low-sodium chicken or vegetable stock

HEAT oil in a Dutch oven or stockpot over medium-high heat. Add ground turkey, onion and garlic. Cook, stirring and breaking up the meat with a wooden spoon, until the meat is no longer pink, 3 to 5 minutes.

ADD zucchini and cook, stirring occasionally, until the zucchini starts to soften, 5 to 7 minutes.

ADD quinoa, oregano, cumin, coriander, pepper and salt and cook, stirring, until aromatic, 30 seconds to 1 minute.

STIR in white beans and chilis, then pour in broth. Bring to a boil.

REDUCE heat to a simmer, partially cover the pot and cook, stirring occasionally, until the liquid is reduced and thickened and the quinoa is tender, about 50 minutes.

NUTRITION FACTS

PER SERVING (1 CUP): 356 CALORIES, 14G FAT, 43MG CHOLESTEROL, 35G CARBS, 26G PROTEIN, 10G FIBER, 722MG SODIUM

Amber Ale Turkey Chili

SERVES 8

1	tbsp + 1 tsp avocado oil
1½	pounds lean ground turkey
1	tsp sea salt
1	large white onion, chopped
4	garlic cloves, minced
2	tbsp chili powder
2	tsp ground cumin
2	tsp dried oregano
1	tsp instant espresso powder
1	12-ounce bottle amber ale (brand of choice)
1	28-ounce can crushed tomatoes
1	15-ounce can fire-roasted diced tomatoes
1	tbsp organic honey
½	tsp red chili pepper flakes
5	15-ounce cans kidney beans, rinsed and rained
1	cup water
–	juice of 1 lime

HEAT 1 tsp oil in a Dutch oven or large stockpot over medium heat. Add turkey and brown, while breaking up meat with a wooden spoon for 5 minutes or until no pink remains. Transfer to a small bowl. Season with salt and set aside.

DRAIN liquid from pan and add remaining oil. Add onion and sauté for 5 minutes or until soft. Add garlic and cook for 1 minute more. Stir in espresso powder, chili powder, cumin and oregano. Sauté for 30 seconds.

POUR in ale and let simmer for 5 minutes. Return turkey to pot and add tomatoes, honey, red chili pepper flakes and 1 cup water. Reduce heat to medium-low. Simmer for 1 hour, stirring occasionally.

ADD beans during last 15 minutes of cooking to heat through, adding a bit more water if needed to cover beans and turkey. Stir in lime juice to finish.

NUTRITION FACTS

PER SERVING (1 CUP): 300 CALORIES, 8G FAT, 35G CARBS, 22G PROTEIN, 5G FIBER, 54MG CALCIUM, 585MG SODIUM

Spicy Chicken Chili

SERVES 7

- 1½ tbsp avocado or coconut oil
- 1 cup red onion, chopped
- 1½ cup bell peppers, chopped
- 1 zucchini, chopped into ½-inch pieces
- 3 garlic cloves, minced
- 1 jalapeño, thinly sliced
- 1 whole roasted chicken, shredded
- 3 tbsp ground chili powder
- 1 tbsp ground cumin
- 1 tbsp dried oregano
- 1 28-ounce can crushed tomatoes
- 1 15-ounce can fire-roasted diced tomatoes
- 1 cup low-sodium chicken stock
- 1 tbsp brown sugar
- 1 tbsp apple cidar vinegar
- 1 tbsp sea salt
- 2 15-ounce cans red kidney beans, rinsed and drained
- 1 15-ounce can cannellini beans, rinsed and drained
- 1 12-ounch bottle of dark beer or ale (brand of choice)

HEAT a large Dutch oven or stockpot over medium heat. Add onion, pepper, zucchini, and jalapeños. Cook until the onion is tender, about 5 minutes. Add garlic and cook for 1 minute.

ADD chili powder, oregano and cumin. Stir well and cook 1 minute. Add beer and let simmer for 5 minutes. Add crushed and diced tomatoes, broth, sugar, vinegar and salt. Bring to a boil, then reduce heat to medium low and simmer covered, stirring often, until the chili is thickened; about 45 minutes.

PREPARE chicken by pulling it off the bone and tearing into small shreds. Add it and the drained, rinsed beans to thickened chili mixture. Simmer another 20 minutes, uncovered.

TOP with a few slices of avocado and chopped fresh cilantro if desired.

Vegan Black Bean Espresso Chili

SERVES 6

- 2 tbsp avocado or coconut oil
- 1 small white onion, chopped
- 1 small red onion, chopped
- 2½ tbsp instant espresso powder
- 2 tbsp ground smoked paprika
- 2 tbsp ground cumin
- 1 28-ounce can crushed tomatoes
- 3 tbsp organic honey
- 3 garlic cloves, minced
- 6 15-ounce cans black beans, rinsed and drained
- 2 or 3 cups water
- 1½ tsp sea salt
- — chili oil to taste
- — pinch ground cinnamon

HEAT oil in Dutch oven or large stockpot over medium-high. Add onions and sauté until translucent.

ADD espresso powder, paprika, cumin, oregano and cook for 1 minute. Add tomatoes, honey and garlic and bring to a simmer. Reduce heat to medium-low, cover and simmer for 30 minutes.

ADD the beans, water, salt, pepper, chili oil and cinnamon. Bring to a boil, and then reduce heat to medium-low and simmer, stirring often, for about 30 minutes until chili thickens.

Paleo Chili

SERVES 6

- 1½ pounds ground beef or bison
- 2 garlic cloves, minced
- 2 tbsp avocado or coconut oil
- 1 medium white onion, diced
- 2 stalks celery, chopped
- 4 medium carrots, peeled and sliced
- 2 medium zucchini, diced
- 2 tbsp ground chili powder
- 1 tsp ground cumin
- 1 tsp dried oregano
- 1 tsp sea salt
- ¼ tsp cayenne pepper (leave out if you don't like spicy)
- 1 15-ounce can fire-roasted crushed tomatoes
- 1 15-ounce can fire-roasted diced tomatoes

BROWN beef/bison over medium heat in large stockpot or Dutch oven until beef is thoroughly cooked and browned. Drain off excess fat, set aside.

ADD oil, onions, celery, carrots and seasonings to the sauté pan and cook until translucent over medium high heat, about 5 to 7 minutes. Once onions are golden and veggies are midway cooked, add garlic and sauté for 1 minute. Add zucchini and cook for 2 minutes, stirring to combine.

ADD cooked beef and tomatoes into the pot and stir well. Bring everything to a boil, stirring frequently, reduce heat and simmer for 20 minutes. Add up to 1 cup of additional liquid such as tomato sauce or water if you prefer to thin out the chili if needed.

TIP! Giving chili a couple of hours rest in the pot after you make it always make it taste better because the flavors have time to meld together. If you can, plan to make the chili well in advance of when you will be eating.

Main Meals

Winner winner. Chicken dinner.

All of the recipes in this section double for lunch or dinner and most make multiple servings so you will have leftovers that will take the prep work down to a manageable level each week.

No-Fail Roast Chicken

SERVES 4

2	medium- to large-sized organic boneless, skinless chicken breasts
–	seasoning of your choice (some of my favorites are ancho chicken and taco seasoning)
4	tbsp water

PREHEAT oven to 350 degrees. Place chicken breasts in foil-lined glass or metal pan. Season as desired and add water to the pan.

BAKE for about 30 minutes or until no longer pink inside. Watch these carefully … it's easy to over-cook them. Let rest for 10 minutes before slicing to let the juices redistribute. Don't skip this important step!

Whole Roasted Chicken

SERVES 8

1	5 or 6 pound roasting chicken
–	sea salt
–	freshly ground black pepper
1	large bunch fresh thyme + 20 sprigs
1	lemon, halved
1	head of garlic, cut in half crosswise
2	tbsp unsalted, grass-fed butter, melted
1	large onion, thickly sliced
4	carrots, cut into 2-inch chunks
1	bulb of fennel, tops removed and cut into wedges
–	extra-virgin olive oil

PREHEAT oven to 425 degrees. Remove the chicken giblets. Rinse the chicken inside and out. Remove any excess fat and leftover pin feathers and pat the outside dry. Liberally salt and pepper the inside of the chicken. Stuff the cavity with the bunch of thyme, both halves of the lemon, and all of the garlic. Brush the outside of the chicken with the butter and sprinkle again with salt and pepper. Tie the legs together with kitchen string and tuck the wing tips under the body of the chicken.

PLACE the onions, carrots, and fennel in a roasting pan. Toss with salt, pepper, 20 sprigs of thyme, and olive oil. Spread around the bottom of the roasting pan and place the chicken on top.

ROAST the chicken for 90 minutes, or until the juices run clear when you cut between a leg and thigh. Remove the chicken and vegetables to a platter and cover with aluminum foil for about 20 minutes. Slice the chicken onto a platter and serve it with the vegetables.

 **TIP!** Save the chicken bones to use in *Chicken Stock* (see *Other Recipes* section).

Feta, Herb & Sun-Dried Tomato Stuffed Chicken

SERVES 4

- 2 cups water
- ½ cup sun-dried tomatoes, packed without oil
- ½ cup crumbled feta cheese
- 2 tsp fresh basil, chopped
- 1 tsp fresh oregano, chopped
- ½ tsp garlic, minced
- ¾ tsp freshly ground black pepper, divided
- 4 6-ounce skinless, boneless chicken breast halves
- ½ tsp sea salt
- 2 tbsp unsalted, grass-fed butter
- ½ tsp lemon zest
- ¼ cup low-sodium chicken broth or stock

PREHEAT oven to 425 degrees. Bring water to a boil in a small saucepan and add tomatoes. Remove from heat, cover and let stand for about 5 minutes. Drain and slice into thin strips. Combine tomatoes, cheese, 2 tsp chopped basil, oregano, garlic and ¼ tsp pepper in a small bowl.

PLACE chicken breast halves between 2 sheets of heavy-duty plastic wrap, and pound each piece to an even thickness using a meat mallet. Cut a horizontal slit through one side of each chicken breast half to form a deep pocket. Stuff ¼ cup tomato mixture into each pocket. Sprinkle both sides of chicken with salt and remaining ½ teaspoon pepper.

FOLD 4 (16 x 12-inch) sheets of heavy-duty foil in half crosswise. Open foil; place 1 tsp butter on half of each foil sheet. Lay one stuffed chicken breast half on top of each portion of butter. Place ⅛ teaspoon lemon zest and on top of each stuffed chicken breast half, and drizzle each serving with 1 tbsp chicken broth or stock. Fold foil over chicken, and tightly seal edges. Place packets on a baking sheet.

BAKE packets for 20 minutes. Remove from oven, and let stand for 5 minutes. Unfold packets carefully, and thinly slice each chicken breast half. Serve immediately.

NUTRITION FACTS

PER SERVING (1 PACKET): 311 CALORIES, 10.1G FAT, 43G PROTEIN, 8.2G CARBS, 2.5G FIBER, 121MG CHOLESTEROL, 572MG SODIUM, 77MG CALCIUM

Grilled Chicken Thighs with Chimichurri Sauce

SERVES 4

- 8 bone-in, skin-on chicken thighs
- 1¼ cup *Chimichurri Sauce*, divided (see *Other Recipes* section)

COAT the chicken in ⅓ cup of the Chimichurri Sauce, and marinate for at least 30 minutes.

PREHEAT grill and cook chicken, skin side down for 6 to 8 minutes. Turn chicken over and grill 4 to 5 minutes until internal temperature reaches 165 degrees.

SERVE with remaining Chimichurri Sauce.

Farrotto with Mushrooms & Vegetables

SERVES 2

- 1¼ cup dry semi-pearled farro
- 2 cups low-sodium vegetable broth or stock
- 1 cup water
- – drizzle extra-virgin olive oil
- ⅓ cup fresh Pecorino Romano or Parmesan cheese, grated
- 1 cup shitake or crimini mushrooms, chopped
- 2 cups baby spinach
- 10 spears asparagus, woody ends removed and chopped in 1-inch pieces
- 1 bunch broccolini, ends trimmed
- – juice of ¼ lemon
- 1 garlic clove, minced
- – freshly ground black pepper to taste

BRING broth and water to a boil in a medium to large saucepan. Add farro and stir. Add salt, pepper and drizzle of extra-virgin olive oil. Let boil for 3 minutes, then reduce heat to medium low and simmer for 15 minutes, or until all the liquid is absorbed.

ADD cheese to the farro and stir until melted. Set aside.

SAUTÉ garlic, asparagus, broccolini and mushrooms lightly in a large sauté pan with a little pepper to taste. Remove from pan and set aside. Sauté 2 cups of spinach with garlic salt and pepper to taste until just wilted (you don't want a a soggy mess!).

MIX farro and vegetables together just before serving.

Quinoa Risotto with Lemon & Roasted Tomatoes

SERVES 4

1½	cups white quinoa, rinsed
–	sea salt
½	cup panko
6	tbsp extra-virgin olive oil
1½	tsp fresh rosemary, minced
2	garlic cloves, minced
–	freshly ground black pepper
4	whole canned Italian tomatoes, drained and halved lengthwise
1	lemon
1	large shallot, finely chopped
2	cups low-sodium chicken or vegetable broth or stock
¼	cup crème fraîche + more for garnish
1	tsp lemon zest
½	cup Parmesan cheese, finely grated
–	flat leaf parsley, chopped

PREHEAT oven to 375 degrees. In a saucepan, bring the quinoa with 2½ cups water and a large pinch of salt to a boil. Cover and cook over low heat until the water is absorbed and the quinoa is tender. Let stand covered for 15 minutes and then fluff with a fork.

MIX the panko with 2 tbsp oil, ½ tsp of the rosemary, half of the garlic and a generous pinch each of salt and pepper in a bowl. Arrange the tomatoes cut side up on a rimmed baking sheet and top with the panko. Bake for 25 minutes until the crumbs are lightly browned and the tomatoes are softened. Keep warm.

PEEL the lemon with a sharp knife, being sure to remove all of the bitter white pith. Working over a bowl, cut in between the membranes to release the sections. Cut the lemon into ¼-inch pieces.

HEAT the remaining oil until shimmering in a medium saucepan. Add the shallot and remaining garlic and cook over moderate heat, stirring until softened, about 4 minutes. Add the remaining rosemary and cook for 1 minute.

STIR in the quinoa and stock and bring just to a boil. Simmer over moderate heat, stirring, until the quinoa is suspended in a thickened sauce, about 5 minutes. Stir in the crème fraîche, lemon zest, lemon sections and ⅓ cup of grated cheese. Season with salt and pepper.

SPOON the risotto into bowls, top with the tomatoes and garnish with a small spoonful of crème fraîche, grated cheese and chopped parsley.

Shrimp & Tomato Risotto

SERVES 4

4	garlic cloves, minced
1¾	cup dry semi-pearled farro
⅓	cup dry white wine
1	carton low-sodium chicken or vegetable stock
1	15-ounce can fire-roasted diced tomatoes
¼	cup Parmesan or Pecorino Romano cheese, freshly grated
2	tbsp basil leaves, sliced
2	to 3 cups baby kale
–	sea salt and freshly ground black pepper to taste

HEAT stock in a large saucepan on low to medium-low heat.

HEAT a large sauté pan on medium heat and toss in farro to toast, 3 to 4 minutes. Remove from pan and set aside.

HEAT oil in the same sauté pan. Add the onion and cook over medium-high heat until softened, about 2 to 3 minutes. Add the garlic and cook 1 minute until fragrant. Add the farro and stir until coated with oil, about 1 minute. Add the white wine and simmer until almost evaporated, about 2 minutes. Lower heat to medium.

SCOOP 1 cup (using a ladle works best) of the heated broth over the farro mixture and cook, stirring, until absorbed. Repeat with remaining broth, adding 1 cup at a time, until the farro is just tender and suspended in a creamy sauce, about 30 minutes total.

STIR in the tomatoes and bring to a boil over medium-high heat. Off the heat, stir in the remaining 1 tbsp of oil and the cheese. Wilt the kale in batches until it's all incorporated.

SEASON with salt and pepper to taste. Spoon into bowls, garnish with basil and a little grated cheese.

Spanish-Style Quinoa with Chicken or Steak

SERVES 8

2	tbsp avocado or coconut oil
1½	cups dry white or red quinoa
1	medium white onion, finely chopped
3	garlic cloves, minced
1	green bell pepper, chopped
1	red bell pepper, chopped
1	cup zucchini, diced
1	cup crushed tomatoes
2½	cups water
1	tsp ground chili powder
¼	tsp garlic powder
¼	tsp ground cumin
–	grated cheese and sliced cherry tomatoes for garnish
3	ounces baked chicken or grilled steak per person

HEAT the oil in a large sauté pan over medium heat. Stir in the quinoa, onion, garlic, peppers and zucchini.

COOK and stir 5 to 10 minutes until onion is tender and the quinoa has lightly toasted. Stir in crushed tomatoes and water, and then season with chili powder, garlic powder and cumin.

BRING to a boil, then reduce heat to medium-low. Cover and simmer until quinoa is tender and liquid is absorbed (about 30 minutes). Stir the quinoa occasionally.

SERVE with chicken or steak and garnish with cheese and tomatoes.

Sweet Potato & Chicken Fajitas

SERVES 4

- 2 small jeweled sweet potatoes, well-scrubbed
- 4 tsp avocado or coconut oil
- 2 Poblano chilis, stemmed, seeded and cut into thin strips
- 1 medium white or red onion, halved and sliced
- 2 boneless, skinless chicken breasts cut into ½-inch thick pieces
- ½ tsp sea salt
- 1 tsp ground cumin
- 1 tsp dried oregano
- ½ cup low-sodium chicken or vegetable broth or stock
- 4 garlic cloves, finely minced
- 8 fajita or taco-sized corn tortillas, warmed
- ½ cup cotija cheese
- ¼ cup fresh cilantro leaves

PIERCE sweet potatoes with a fork and microwave on high until almost tender when pierced with a knife, about 3 minutes. Cool completely. Halve lengthwise, and then slice each half diagonally into ½-inch thick pieces.

HEAT 2 tsp oil in a large sauté pan over medium heat. Add chilis and sauté until softened slightly, about 8 minutes. Add onion and sweet potatoes and sauté until golden brown, about 8 minutes. Transfer vegetables into a large bowl.

HEAT the remaining oil in the same pan. Add chicken and sprinkle with salt, cumin and oregano. Sauté until chicken is browned and cooked through, about 6 minutes. Return vegetables to pan; add garlic and broth and simmer until liquid is almost evaporated, about 2 minutes.

DIVIDE fajita mixture among tortillas. Sprinkle with cheese and cilantro.

NUTRITION FACTS

PER SERVING: 406 CALORIES, 26G PROTEIN, 47G CARBS, 15G FAT, 7G FIBER, 504 MG SODIUM

Chili-Rubbed Steak Tacos

SERVES 6

- 1 tbsp ground chili powder
- 2 cloves garlic, minced
- ¼ tsp ground cinnamon
- ¼ tsp sea salt
- – pinch of cayenne pepper
- 1¼ pound top sirloin steaks, cut 1-inch thick
- 12 fajita or taco-sized corn tortillas, warmed
- 3 cups red cabbage, shredded or chopped
- 1 lime, cut into wedges
- 2 cups *Avocado Lime Salsa* (see *Condiments & Dressings* section)

STIR together chili powder, garlic, cinnamon, salt and cayenne pepper in a small bowl. Rub spice mixture on both sides of steaks.

GRILL OR BROIL steaks for 5 to 6 minutes on each side for medium rare, turning once.

REMOVE from grill and let meat sit for 10 to 15 minutes. Carve into thin slices.

WARM tortillas by placing them on the grill, for about 30 seconds, turning once. Or place six tortillas at a time between two moist paper towels and microwave for 45 seconds. Wrap in cloth napkin or place in a tortilla warmer to keep warm.

ASSEMBLE the tacos with beef, cabbage and salsa.

NUTRITION FACTS

PER SERVING (2 TACOS): 386 CALORIES, 16G FAT, 21G PROTEIN, 41G CARBS, 4G SUGAR, 8G FIBER, 258MG SODIUM

Turkey Taco Lettuce Cups

SERVES 6

- 4 tbsp avocado oil, divided
- 4 garlic cloves, minced
- 2 medium-sized zucchini squash, diced into small chunks
- 2 bell peppers (any color), diced into chunks
- 1 medium red onion, diced
- 1½ pounds lean ground turkey
- — sea salt and freshly ground black pepper to taste
- 4 tbsp taco seasoning
- — butter or romaine lettuce leaves, rinsed and patted dry
- — *Traditional Guacamole* (see *Condiments & Dressings* section), *Pico de Gallo* or store-bought salsa for serving

HEAT a large sauté pan over medium-high heat. Add 2 tbsp oil and ground meat. Break meat up into small chunks. Season with salt and pepper. Cook meat until brown (about 6 to 8 minutes). Stir in 2 tbsp taco seasoning, then transfer to a strainer to drain away excess fat.

ADD remaining oil to pan. Add garlic, onion, and all chopped veggies. Lightly salt and pepper. Add remaining taco seasoning. Stir, cooking vegetables, onion and garlic until softened (about 5 minutes). Add meat to veggie mixture and stir to combine.

CLEAN and prepare butter or romaine lettuce leaves. Spoon taco mixture onto lettuce. Top with guacamole and salsa.

TIP! The leftover taco mixture can be used over a salad with Smoky Barbecue Dressing (see *Condiments & Dressings* section), or for breakfast with scrambled, fried or poached eggs

Herbed Turkey Burgers

SERVES 2

- — cooking spray
- ½ pound lean ground turkey
- 1 tbsp fresh parsley, chopped
- 1 tbsp fresh chives, chopped
- 1 garlic clove, minced
- ¼ tsp sea salt
- ¼ tsp freshly ground black pepper
- ½ large tomato, sliced into ¼-inch rounds
- ¼ medium zucchini, sliced into ¼-inch rounds
- ½ medium red onion, sliced into ¼-inch rounds
- 2 whole wheat or sprouted grain hamburger buns
- — condiments of choice (such as mixed greens or lettuce, avocado, mustard, etc.)

COAT grill pan with cooking spray, then heat into medium-high. In a medium bowl, combine turkey, parsley, chives, garlic, salt, and pepper until well mixed. Form into four patties, each about ½-inch thick, and place on grill pan.

COOK for 2 to 3 minutes, then turn and cook for 2 minutes more or until cooked through. Remove from grill and transfer to a plate to rest and let juices settle.

PLACE tomato, zucchini and onion slices on heated grill pan and cook, flipping once midway through for 2 to 4 minutes or until tender.

PLACE each burger on a bun bottom, then top each evenly with the grilled tomatoes, zucchini and onions. Cover with the remaining bun halves and serve with other desired condiments or toppings.

NUTRITIONAL FACTS

PER SERVING (1 BURGER + VEGGIES):
338 CALORIES, 11G FAT, 34G CARBS, 30G PROTEIN, 6G FIBER, 64MG CALCIUM, 3MG IRON, 553MG SODIUM

Veggie Burgers

SERVES 6

- 4 tsp avocado or coconut oil
- 1 medium red or white onion, small dice
- 3 garlic cloves, minced
- 2 carrots, finely grated
- 1 yellow zucchini, grated
- 1 green zucchini, grated
- 1 tsp sea salt
- ¼ tsp freshly ground black pepper
- 1 tsp ground paprika
- 2 tbsp flat leaf parsley, chopped
- 1 large organic omega-3 egg, beaten
- 1½ cups rolled oats
- ¼ cup canned black beans, rinsed and drained
- – all-purpose flour for dusting
- 6 whole wheat or sprouted grain hamburger buns
- – condiments of choice (such as mixed greens or lettuce, avocado, mustard, red onion, etc)

HEAT 2 tsp oil in a large sauté pan over medium-high. Add onion and reduce heat to medium. Add the garlic and sauté for 3 to 4 minutes until soft. Mix in carrots, squash, zucchini, salt and pepper. Cook for 3 to 4 minutes more, or until soft. Mix in black beans, egg, paprika, parsley and oats. Remove from heat, transfer to a bowl and let rest at room temp for 1 hour.

DIVIDE the mixture to 6 equal parts and form each into a flattened, round patty. Lightly coat each side with flour.

HEAT remaining 2 tsp oil in a sauté pan over medium-high. Add patties and cook for 3 to 4 minutes on each side, or until golden brown.

SERVE on buns topped with condiments of choice.

NUTRITION FACTS

PER SERVING (1 BURGER + BUN):
291 CALORIES, 8G FAT (1G SATURATED),
48G CARBS, 12G PROTEIN, 8G FIBER,
80MG CALCIUM, 3MG IRON, 577MG SODIUM

Lemon-Roasted Salmon

SERVES 2

2	5-ounce wild-caught salmon fillets
–	regular or lemon-flavored olive oil
–	zest of ½ lemon
–	sea salt to taste
–	freshly ground black pepper to taste

PREHEAT oven to 425 degrees. Line a baking sheet with a square of foil, and crimp up the ends so that it forms a barrier so that any liquid does not leak in your oven.

PREP salmon fillet with salt, pepper, oil and zest. Add a slice of lemon to the top. Place salmon skin side down on the foil.

BAKE for 12 minutes. Remove from oven and allow to rest for 3 to 5 minutes.

SLIDE spatula between salmon and skin to remove from baking sheet.

Pistachio & Broccoli Crusted Salmon

SERVES 4

4	5-ounce wild-caught salmon fillets
¾	cup unsalted pistachios, shelled
1	garlic clove, minced
¼	tsp sea salt
⅔	cup broccoli florets, stems trimmed
1	cup fresh basil leaves

PREHEAT oven to 425 degrees. Line a baking sheet with parchment paper and set aside.

PLACE pistachios in a food processor and pulse until roughly chopped. Transfer to a bowl and set aside. Add garlic, broccoli, basil, oil and 1 tsp water to food processor and pulse until consistency is of a thick, chunky pureé. Add more water if necessary.

PUT salmon fillets on prepared baking sheet, skin side down. Use a spoon to evenly distribute the pesto over the fillets and top each with a quarter of the crushed pistachios. Bake for 12 minutes, or until salmon is just pink. Remove from oven and let rest for 3 to 5 minutes.

SLIDE spatula between salmon and skin to remove from baking sheet.

Citrusy Salmon with Kale & Barley

SERVES 2

- 1 cup water
- ½ cup fresh squeezed orange juice
- 1 tsp fresh ginger, finely chopped
- ½ tsp reduced-sodium soy sauce or Bragg's liquid aminos
- 2 4-ounce wild-caught salmon fillets, skin removed
- 3 cups green curly kale, de-stemmed and chopped
- 1 cup barley (sub in farro if desired)
- – sea salt
- – freshly ground black pepper
- 1 tsp extra-virgin olive oil

PREPARE barley according to package directions. Drain and set aside.

BRING water, orange juice, ginger and soy sauce/Bragg's LA over medium-high heat in a medium sauté pan.

ADD salmon fillets; simmer, covered, until salmon is opaque, about 10 minutes. Remove salmon and set aside; bring liquid to a boil and cook until reduced by half, 2 minutes.

ADD 3 cups kale; cook until kale is wilted, 2 minutes.

SLIDE ½ cup cooked barley with 1 tsp olive oil and a pinch of salt and black pepper in a bowl. Serve salmon, kale and any remaining cooking liquid with barley.

NUTRITION FACTS

PER SERVING (1 SALMON FILLET, ¾ CUP BARLEY AND KALE MIXTURE): 455 CALORIES, 14G FAT, 55G CARBS, 7G FIBER, 32G PROTEIN

Couscous with Shrimp & Green Beans

SERVES 6

- 2 cups low-sodium chicken or vegetable broth or stock
- 4 ounces fresh green beans, trimmed and cut into ½-inch lengths
- 1 tsp ground curry powder
- ⅛ tsp dried red pepper flakes
- 30 medium to large shrimp, peeled and deveined
- 1 cup dry whole wheat couscous
- 1 cup frozen artichoke hearts, thawed and coarsely chopped
- ½ cup frozen peas
- ⅔ cup grape or cherry tomatoes, halved lengthwise
- 2 tbsp fresh basil, minced
- – sea salt
- – freshly ground black pepper

COMBINE broth, green beans, curry powder, red pepper flakes in a large sauté pan. Bring them to a boil on high heat.

ADD the shrimp and reduce heat to medium. Cook for 1 minute or until shrimp begin to turn pink.

ADD couscous, artichokes and peas; stir just enough so the couscous is covered with broth. Cover and remove from heat. Let stand for 5 to 6 minutes or until the liquid is absorbed. Add the tomatoes and the basil and gently toss.

TASTE and season with salt and pepper as desired.

NUTRITION FACTS

PER SERVING: 150 CALORIES, 1.5G FAT, 21G CARBS, 230MG SODIUM, 5G FIBER, 2G SUGAR, 15G PROTEIN

Garlicky Shrimp

SERVES 4

- ¼ cup olive oil
- 4 garlic cloves, finely minced
- ¼ tsp red pepper flakes
- ¼ cup fresh flat-leaf parsley, minced
- 30 medium to large shrimp, peeled and deveined

HEAT olive oil on medium-high until shimmering in a large sauté pan. Add the garlic, red pepper flakes and parsley and cook for 10 seconds, stirring.

ADD shrimp and cook, turning once, until they are pink and curled, 2 to 3 minutes each side. Shrimp cook really quickly so keep a close eye on these!

TIP! You can serve this with crusty bread to soak up the remaining cooking oil (if you do this, add another ¼ cup oil when cooking) and a bunch of grilled vegetables. I have also served these over a green salad with tomatoes, red onions, grilled asparagus and the *Simple Vinaigrette Dressing*.

Chermoula Fish Fillets

SERVES 6

- 3 garlic cloves
- 1½ cups loosely packed fresh cilantro (leaves and tender stems)
- 1½ cups loosely packed fresh flat-leaf parsley (leaves and tender stems)
- – zest and juice of 1 lemon, divided
- 6 tbsp plain full-fat Greek yogurt
- 1 tbsp extra-virgin olive oil
- 1½ tsp ground sweet or smoked paprika
- 1 tsp ground cumin
- ⅛ tsp ground cayenne pepper
- ½ tsp sea salt + additional to taste
- – cooking spray
- 4 5-ounce firm white fish fillets (such as halibut or cod) about ¾-inch thick
- ½ tsp freshly ground black pepper

PREPARE chermoula by blending garlic, cilantro, parsley and lemon zest in a food processor until finely chopped. Add yogurt, lemon juice, oil, paprika, cumin and cayenne and process to incorporate. Add salt to taste and set aside.

MIST a shallow baking dish or large foil-lined baking sheet with cooking spray. Spread about half of chermoula on both sides or over top of fish, and then sprinkle with salt and pepper. Arrange fish in baking dish or on sheet in a single layer and set aside at room temperature for 15 to 30 minutes.

ARRANGE oven rack about 4 inches from heat source and preheat broiler to high.

BROIL fish until just cooked through for 5 to 7 minutes. Transfer to serving plates and drizzle with any cooking juices. Serve remaining chermoula on the side.

NUTRITION FACTS

PER SERVING (1 FISH FILLET AND 2½ TBSP CHERMOULA): 192 CALORIES, 6G FAT, 6G CARBS, 2G FIBER, 2G SUGAR, 26G PROTEIN, 367MG SODIUM, 69MG CHOLESTEROL

Halibut with Lentils & Mustard Sauce

SERVES 4

- 2 tbsp extra-virgin olive oil
- 1 large white onion, chopped
- 2 garlic cloves, chopped
- 1 medium jeweled sweet potato, peeled and cut into ¼-inch pieces
- 1¼ cups green lentils, rinsed
- — sea salt and freshly ground black pepper
- 4 6-ounce halibut fillets
- ¼ cup Dijon mustard
- ¼ cup dry white wine
- 1 tbsp fresh tarragon, chopped

HEAT 1 tbsp of the oil in a large saucepan over medium heat. Add the onion and cook, stirring occasionally, until soft, 5 to 6 minutes.

ADD garlic and sweet potato and cook, stirring, for 1 minute.

ADD broth and lentils and simmer, covered, until the lentils are tender, 20 to 25 minutes. Season with ½ teaspoon each salt and pepper.

HEAT remaining oil in a sauté pan over medium-high heat. Season the fish with ¼ teaspoon each salt and pepper. Cook until opaque throughout, 3 to 5 minutes per side.

WHISK together the mustard, wine, and tarragon in a bowl. Divide the lentil mixture and fish among plates and drizzle with the sauce.

Fennel-Crusted Pork Loin with Potatoes & Pears

SERVES 4

- 1 tbsp fennel seeds
- 2 garlic cloves, minced
- 4 tbsp extra-virgin olive oil
- — sea salt and freshly ground black pepper
- 2 pounds boneless pork loin
- 2 red onions, quartered
- 1 pound small white or red potatoes, quartered
- 3 firm pears (such as Bartlett), cored and quartered
- 1 bulb fennel, core removed, sliced

PREHEAT oven to 400 degrees. Gently crush fennel seeds using a mortar and pestle or spice grinder. In a small bowl, mix the seeds, the garlic, 2 tbsp of the oil, 1 tsp salt, and ¼ teaspoon pepper. Rub the mixture over the pork, and then place the pork in a large roasting pan.

TOSS onions, potatoes, fennel, pears, 1 tsp salt and ¼ teaspoon pepper with remaining oil in a bowl. Scatter around the pork and roast until cooked through until internal temperature reaches 160 degrees (keep an eye on it!). Transfer the pork to a cutting board and let rest at least 5 minutes before slicing. Serve with the roasted fruit and vegetables.

Herb-Crusted Pork Loin

SERVES 6 TO 8

- 3 pound boneless pork loin roast
- 2 tbsp freshly ground black pepper
- 2 tbsp Parmesan cheese, freshly grated
- 2 tsp dried basil
- 2 tsp dried rosemary
- 2 tsp dried thyme
- ¼ tsp garlic powder
- ¼ tsp sea salt

PREHEAT oven to 350 degrees.

PAT pork dry with paper towel. In small bowl, mix all rub ingredients well and apply to all surfaces of the pork roast.

PLACE roast in a shallow pan and roast for 1 hour (20 minutes per pound), until internal temperature on a thermometer reads 160 degrees.

REMOVE roast from oven; let rest about 10 minutes before slicing to serve.

NUTRITION FACTS
PER SERVING: 200 CALORIES, 25G PROTEIN, 10G FAT, 115MG SODIUM, 75MG CHOLESTEROL, 1G CARBS, 1G FIBER

Beef Tagine with Butternut Squash

SERVES 4

- 2 tsp ground sweet or smoked paprika
- 1 tsp ground cinnamon
- ¾ tsp sea salt
- ½ tsp ground ginger
- ½ tsp red pepper flakes
- ¼ tsp freshly ground black pepper
- 1 pound beef shoulder roast or petite tender roast, trimmed and cut into 1-inch cubes
- 1 tbsp avocado or coconut oil
- 4 shallots, quartered
- 4 garlic cloves, minced
- ½ cup low-sodium chicken broth or stock
- 1 15-ounce can diced tomatoes, undrained
- 3 cups butternut squash, peeled and cubed into 1-inch pieces (buy pre-done from the store to save time)
- ¼ cup fresh cilantro, chopped

COMBINE first six ingredients in a medium bowl. Add beef; toss well to coat.

HEAT oil in a Dutch oven or large sauté pan over medium-high heat. Add beef and shallots; cook 4 minutes or until browned, stirring occasionally. Add garlic; cook 1 minute, stirring frequently. Stir in broth and tomatoes; bring to a boil. Cook 5 minutes. Add squash; cover, reduce heat and simmer 15 minutes or until squash is tender. Sprinkle with cilantro.

Sirloin Steak with Garlic Butter

SERVES 2

- 2 tbsp unsalted, grass-fed butter, at room temperature
- ½ tsp garlic powder
- 1 garlic clove, minced
- 2 4-ounce beef top sirloin steaks
- – sea salt and freshly ground black pepper to taste

PREHEAT oven to 350 degrees.

ADD a drizzle olive or avocado oil to an oven-safe sauté pan, and pan-sear your steaks over medium-high heat for 1 to 2 minutes each side to get that delicious crust.

PLACE the pan on the oven rack closest to the broiler. Cooking times will vary between 3 to 18 minutes, depending on the thickness of your steak and how you like it cooked. For medium rare, I usually cook for about 8 minutes. Keep checking it until it gets to your desired state.

MIX butter and garlic powder together in a small bowl and set aside.

TRANSFER steak to a warmed plate and brush tops liberally with garlic butter and allow the meat to rest 5 minutes before serving.

Pepper-Crusted Beef Tenderloin

SERVES 6 TO 8

- 6 tbsp mixed peppercorns, coarsely ground
- 1 cup loosely packed fresh flat-leaf parsley, finely chopped + fresh parsley for garnish
- 3 tbsp Dijon mustard
- 2 tbsp unsalted, grass-fed butter, at room temperature
- – sea salt
- 3 pounds center-cut, grass-fed beef tenderloin, trimmed and tied if uneven

PREPARE the peppercorns in a spice or coffee grinder and transfer to a medium bowl. Add the parsley, mustard, butter and 1 tbsp salt to the bowl and mix together until thoroughly combined. Rub the spiced butter all over the tenderloin, rolling the beef in the portions that fall off to coat completely. Be careful not to make it too thick—the rub is very peppery and will be too much to eat if too thick. The beef can be prepared up to this point, covered, and refrigerated up to 1 day in advance.

PREHEAT oven to 450 degrees. Place the beef on a rack and set over a baking sheet. Roast until a meat thermometer inserted into the center registers 130 degrees for medium rare, about 35 to 40 minutes. Remove from the oven and let stand for 10 minutes. Transfer the beef to a cutting board, preferably a meat board with a reservoir to catch the juices, and garnish with the parsley.

Coconut Ginger Chicken with Rice & Vegetables

SERVES 6 TO 8

4	garlic cloves, peeled
2	inches cube of ginger, roughly chopped
1	small sweet onion, peeled, quartered
1	tbsp avocado or coconut oil
2	tbsp unsalted grass-fed butter
2½	pounds boneless, skinless chicken thighs, cut into 4 pieces
2	cans coconut milk, not shaken (look for BPA-free label; sub in "lite" version if desired)
1	cup peas or frozen vegetables of your choice
1	can of baby corn cobbs
2	tbsp corn starch

Spice Blend

½	tsp fresh basil, thinly sliced
1	tsp ground cumin
1	tsp ground coriander
1½	tsp ground turmeric
1	tsp sea salt

COMBINE ingredients from the spice blend together and set aside.

COMBINE garlic, ginger and onion (aromatics) in a mini food processor and pulse until it forms a paste.

PLACE slow cooker on a burner, heat oil and melt butter over medium heat. Add pureéd aromatics and stir well. Cook for a few minutes, then add spice blend. Cook for 2 to 3 minutes, stirring constantly.

MOVE aromatics to one side of the pot and add chicken pieces to the pot. Cook chicken slightly on all sides, using a sturdy wooden spoon to move it around the pot. It should get thoroughly coated with the spice mixture.

OPEN the cans of coconut milk, spoon out the cream from the top and set aside. You should have about 1 cup of milk left. Pour the coconut milk over the chicken and with both cans, it should just barely cover the chicken.

PLACE the slow cooker in the base and cook on low for 4 hours.

WHISK cornstarch with coconut cream until smooth and add to the chicken. Stir well. Add frozen peas, corn cobbs and/or other vegetables of your choice. Cook for another 30 minutes or until chicken is cooked to your liking and the vegetables hot.

SERVE over brown rice, couscous, farro or any of the *Cauliflower Rice* varieties you like.

TIP! Use boneless, skinless chicken breasts in place of the thighs if you prefer. You can also use any cooked or frozen vegetables you have on hand. And if you prefer something spicier, double the ginger and add a ½ tsp of chili flakes.

Green Chicken Curry

SERVES 4

- 2 tbsp avocado or coconut oil
- 1 pound boneless, skinless chicken thighs, trimmed, cut into bite-size pieces
- 1 bunch scallions, sliced
- 1 medium jeweled sweet potato, cut into ½-inch cubes
- 1½ cups halved green beans, fresh or frozen (thawed)
- 1 15-ounce can "lite" coconut milk (look for BPA-free label)
- 2 tbsp Thai green, red or yellow curry paste
- 1 tbsp fish sauce
- 3 cups bok choy, sliced
- ¼ cup fresh basil, chopped
- 1 tsp fresh lime juice

HEAT oil in a large sauté pan over medium-high heat. Add chicken and scallions and cook, stirring, until the chicken is no longer pink, 4 to 5 minutes. Transfer to a plate with a slotted spoon.

ADD sweet potato to the pan and cook, stirring, for 2 minutes. Add coconut milk, curry paste, fish sauce, bok choy and green beans; bring to a simmer. Reduce heat to medium, cover and cook, stirring once or twice, until the vegetables are tender, 5 to 7 minutes.

RETURN the chicken and any accumulated juices to the pan and cook until heated through, about 2 minutes more. Remove from heat and stir in basil and lime juice.

SERVE over brown rice, couscous, farro or any of the *Cauliflower Rice* varieties you like.

NUTRITION FACTS

PER SERVING (1¼ CUP): 358 CALORIES, 20G FAT, 106MG CHOLESTEROL, 20G CARBS, 0G ADDED SUGAR, 24G PROTEIN, 4G FIBER, 604MG SODIUM

Indian Dal

SERVES 4

- 3 tbsp avocado or coconut oil
- 1 tsp mustard seeds
- 1 tsp fresh ginger, grated
- 2 garlic cloves, minced
- 1 white onion, chopped
- 5 medium carrots, chopped
- 5 celery stalks, chopped
- 2 tsp ground coriander
- 1 tsp turmeric
- 1 tsp ground cumin
- 1 tsp ground cayenne pepper
- ½ tsp ground cinnamon
- ½ tsp ground cloves
- 1½ cups red lentils, rinsed
- 4 cups low-sodium vegetable broth or stock (sub water if desired)
- 1 15-ounce can diced tomatoes
- 1 tsp sea salt
- 1 lime, juiced
- ½ cup fresh cilantro, chopped

HEAT oil in a large sauté pan or Dutch oven over high heat. Add the mustard seeds and fry until they begin to pop, about 1 minute. Reduce the heat to medium and add the ginger, garlic, onion, carrots, and celery. Cook until the vegetables just begin to soften, about 5 minutes.

ADD coriander, turmeric, cumin, cayenne, cinnamon, and cloves and stir to combine.

ADD rinsed lentils, stock or water, diced tomatoes, and salt. Stir, and bring to a boil. Reduce heat and simmer, covered, stirring occasionally, for about 15 to 20 minutes, or until the lentils are done and the soup has thickened.

ADD lime juice, cilantro, and salt to taste before serving.

Terriyaki Salmon & Asparagus Stir Fry

SERVES 4

1	cup dry brown rice
1½	cups water
2	tsp avocado or coconut oil
1	pound skinless salmon, thinly sliced
1	bunch asparagus, woody ends trimmed, sliced in 1-inch pieces
⅓	cup teriyaki sauce
1	tbsp Sriracha hot sauce
1	tbsp fresh ginger, minced
2	garlic cloves, minced
1	tbsp sesame seeds (white or black)
2	tbsp fresh flat-leaf parsley, chopped

ADD rice and water in a medium saucepan. Bring to a boil, reduce heat to low and simmer covered until rice is tender, about 25 minutes. Remove from heat and let stand covered for five minutes. Fluff with a fork and set aside.

HEAT a stir-fry pan or large sauté pan over medium-high heat. Add oil and swirl to coat pan. Add salmon pieces and cook 2 minutes, or until just beginning to turn opaque. Remove salmon from pan and set aside.

PLACE asparagus in pan and cook 2 minutes or until asparagus is tender-crisp, stirring often.

STIR together teriyaki sauce, Sriracha, ginger and garlic. Return salmon to pan along with teriyaki mixture, stir to coat and heat 1 minute.

SERVE over brown rice and garnish with sesame seeds and fresh parsley.

NUTRITION FACTS

PER SERVING: 489 CALORIES, 20G FAT, 364MG SODIUM, 46G CARBS, 5G FIBER, 6G SUGAR, 31G PROTEIN

Chicken & Broccoli Stir Fry

SERVES 4

- ½ tbsp avocado or coconut oil
- 3 lean, skinless and boneless chicken breasts, cut into strips 1-inch thick
- ½ medium white onion, sliced
- 2 cups broccoli florets
- 1 cup carrots, julienned
- 1 cup mushrooms, sliced
- 2 garlic cloves, minced
- ½ tbsp peanut or almond butter
- 1 tbsp low-sodium soy sauce or Bragg's liquid aminos
- ½ tsp Sriracha hot sauce
- 2 dashes fish sauce
- ¼ tsp sesame oil
- ¼ tsp red pepper flakes
- ⅛ tsp sesame seeds (white or black)

ADD oil to a stir-fry pan or large sauté pan over medium-high heat and add chicken, sautéing until fully cooked, 4 minutes on each side. Take out of the pan and set aside.

HEAT another ½ tbsp of oil in the same pan and add onions, broccoli, carrots and mushrooms. Sauté for 3 to 4 minutes until slightly tender. Add in garlic and sauté for 1 minute.

STIR in nut butter, soy sauce, Sriracha, fish sauce, sesame oil, red pepper flakes and sesame seeds. Bring to a low simmer and cook for 1 to 2 minutes.

SLICE cooked chicken and add back into the pan. Toss to coat the chicken. Cook until chicken is warmed through, about 1 or 2 minutes.

GARNISH with extra sesame seeds and serve immediately.

Dessert

Because life can always be sweeter …

Dessert is one of life's pleasures and you should be able to enjoy eating it. The recipes in this section are healthier options that taste really good, aren't too heavy on the sugar or calories and incorporate fruits and vegetables such as berries, stone fruit, avocado and zucchini wherever possible.

If you just want something quick, easy and yummy, I also recommend good quality dark chocolate (look for 70% cocoa content and less than 10g sugar per serving if possible) or fresh berries or fruit like raspberries or strawberries. Fresh, in-season stone fruit also hits the spot!

Spiced Peach & Pistachio Crisp

SERVES 6

- 5 medium peaches, peeled, pitted and sliced
- 2 tbsp organic honey
- ½ cup + 1 tsp whole wheat flour
- ½ tsp cinnamon
- ½ cup rolled oats
- ¼ cup packed brown sugar
- ¼ cup shelled pistachios, chopped
- 1 tsp ground ginger
- ¼ tsp ground cardamom
- ¼ tsp sea salt
- 4 tbsp unsalted grass-fed butter, melted

PREHEAT oven to 350 degrees. In a large mixing bowl, combine peaches, honey, 1 tsp flour and cinnamon.

WHISK together oats, remaining flour, brown sugar, pistachios, ginger, cardamom and salt in a medium-sized mixing bowl. Using a wooden spoon, mix in butter and stir until oat mixture is moistened.

POUR peach filling into a 1-quart baking dish and top with oat mixture. Bake for 35 minutes or until filling bubbles around edges and a knife inserted into the center meets no resistance. Let rest 10 minutes before serving.

NUTRITION FACTS

PER SERVING: 249 CALORIES, 5G PROTEIN, 41G CARBS, 9G FAT, 5G FIBER, 152MG SODIUM

Apple & Pear Crisp

SERVES 2

- 1 small Bartlett or D'anjou pear, cored and diced
- 1 small Granny Smith apple, cored and diced
- ½ tbsp fresh lemon juice
- ½ cup rolled oats
- ¼ cup whole wheat flour
- ¼ tsp ground cinnamon
- ¼ tsp ground ginger
- – pinch ground nutmeg
- 2 tbsp pure maple syrup
- 1½ tbsp coconut oil, melted

PREHEAT oven to 375 degrees. In a small bowl, mix together pears, apples, 1 tbsp maple syrup, and lemon juice. Place fruit filling in two 6-ounce ramekins.

MIX together topping ingredients in a separate bowl until well blended. Topping should be moist and crumbly. Sprinkle mixture on top of filling. Bake for 20 minutes or until golden brown.

NUTRITION FACTS

PER SERVING: 375 CALORIES, 60G CARBS, 8G FIBER, 12G FAT, 6G PROTEIN, 51MG CALCIUM, 2MG IRON

Baked Fruit Crumble

SERVES 6

- 1½ cup raspberries
- 3 ripe apricots, pitted and chopped
- 2 tsp lemon juice
- 1 tbsp pure maple syrup or organic honey
- – pinch ground cloves
- 8 tbsp rolled oats
- 4 tbsp whole wheat flour
- – pinch sea salt
- 4 tsp real vanilla extract or ground vanilla
- 3 tbsp coconut oil, room temperature

PREHEAT oven to 375. Line an oven rack with foil. Prepare the fruit. Place raspberries and chopped apricots in a mixing bowl. Add lemon juice, maple syrup or honey and cloves, tossing with your hands to combine. Spoon the fruit mixture equally into 6 ramekins (you could also use a small glass baking dish if desired).

PREPARE the crumble by mixing oats, flour and salt in a mixing bowl. Then add vanilla and coconut oil and mix with your fingers. It should resemble a loose, crumbly dough. Place evenly in the ramekins on top of the fruit filling.

BAKE for 20 minutes until top is golden and fruit juice is bubbling. Let cool for a few minutes before serving.

Pear, Fig & Pecan Galette

SERVES 4

- 1 sheet frozen puff pastry dough or pie dough (flat), thawed
- 2 small pears, cored and thinly sliced
- 1 tsp unsalted grass-fed butter
- ½ tsp ground cinnamon
- ½ tsp ground cloves
- ¼ tsp ground nutmeg
- 1½ tbsp whole wheat flour
- 1½ tbsp brown sugar
- 1 organic omega-3 egg, gently beaten
- 4 tbsp fig jam
- ¼ cup raw pecans, rough chopped

PLACE an oven rack to the center of the oven and preheat to 375 degrees. Mix sugar, flour, cinnamon, nutmeg and cloves together in a bowl until well combined; stir in the sliced pears and coat.

LINE a baking sheet with a silpat or parchment paper, lay out dough and poke several holes in the bottom of the crust. Spread the fig jam on the dough, leaving a 1½-inch border. Sprinkle chopped pecans over the jam. Lay the pear slices in a tight circle starting with the outer border of the jam, adding a few of the leftovers in the middle to completely cover the jam and dough. Crimp the edges of the pastry over. It will not completely cover the pears, just the outer 1 to 2 inches.

TOP the exposed mixture with cold butter. Brush edges with beaten egg to help the crust get golden brown and crispy.

BAKE about 30 minutes, until the pastry is puffed and brown and the pears are tender when pierced with a toothpick. Let cool for 5 to 10 minutes, and serve immediately.

Summer Peach/Plum Crostata

SERVES 4

- 1¼ cups all-purpose or whole wheat flour + more for dusting
- ½ cup sugar + more for sprinkling
- ¼ tsp sea salt
- 1 stick unsalted grass-fed butter, cubed and chilled
- ¼ cup ice water
- 1 large organic omega-3 egg yolk mixed with 1 tbsp of water

Fruit Mixture
- 1 tbsp cornstarch
- ¼ tsp ground cinnamon
- ¼ tsp finely grated orange zest
- ½ pound firm but ripe plums, pitted and cut into eighths OR ½ pound firm but ripe peaches, pitted and cut into eighths

ADD flour, 2 tbsp of sugar and salt to food processor and pulse to combine. Add the butter and pulse until the mixture resembles coarse meal. Sprinkle in ice water and pulse until the dough just barely comes together. Gather the dough and pat it into a disk. Wrap the dough in plastic and refrigerate until chilled, about 30 minutes. If you don't feel like making your own dough, purchase a pre-made pie crust (flat, not in a pan) in your store's freezer section.

PREHEAT oven to 425 degrees and position a rack in the lower third. Line a baking sheet with a silpat or parchment paper. Working on a lightly floured surface, roll out the disk of dough to a 12-inch round; transfer to the baking sheet. Chill the dough until firm, 15 minutes.

COMBINE remaining ¼ cup plus 2 tbsp of sugar in a bowl with the cornstarch, cinnamon and orange zest. Add the fruit and toss well. Let stand, stirring occasionally, until the sugar is mostly dissolved, about 15 minutes.

ARRANGE fruit in the center of the dough, leaving a 1½-inch border all around. Fold the edge of the dough up and over the fruit. Brush the rim with the egg wash and sprinkle with sugar.

BAKE crostata for about 50 minutes, until the crust is golden and the fruit is tender and bubbling. Let it cool on the baking sheet for 30 minutes, then cut into wedges and serve.

Chocolate Mousse

SERVES 2

- 1 large ripe avocado, peeled and pitted
- 2 tsp cacao powder (unsweetened cocoa powder is fine, too)
- 1 tsp Stevia or Truvia
- 1 tbsp pure maple syrup or organic honey
- ⅓ cup coconut cream (spoon out the thick cream on the top of a BPA-free can of coconut milk)
- ¼ cup dark chocolate chips
- ¼ cup fresh raspberries

USE the chopper/grinder attachment that comes with most immersion blenders to blend all ingredients. A regular blender works too.

LET it set for about 30 minutes in the refrigerator. Spoon into individual serving dishes and top with raspberries.

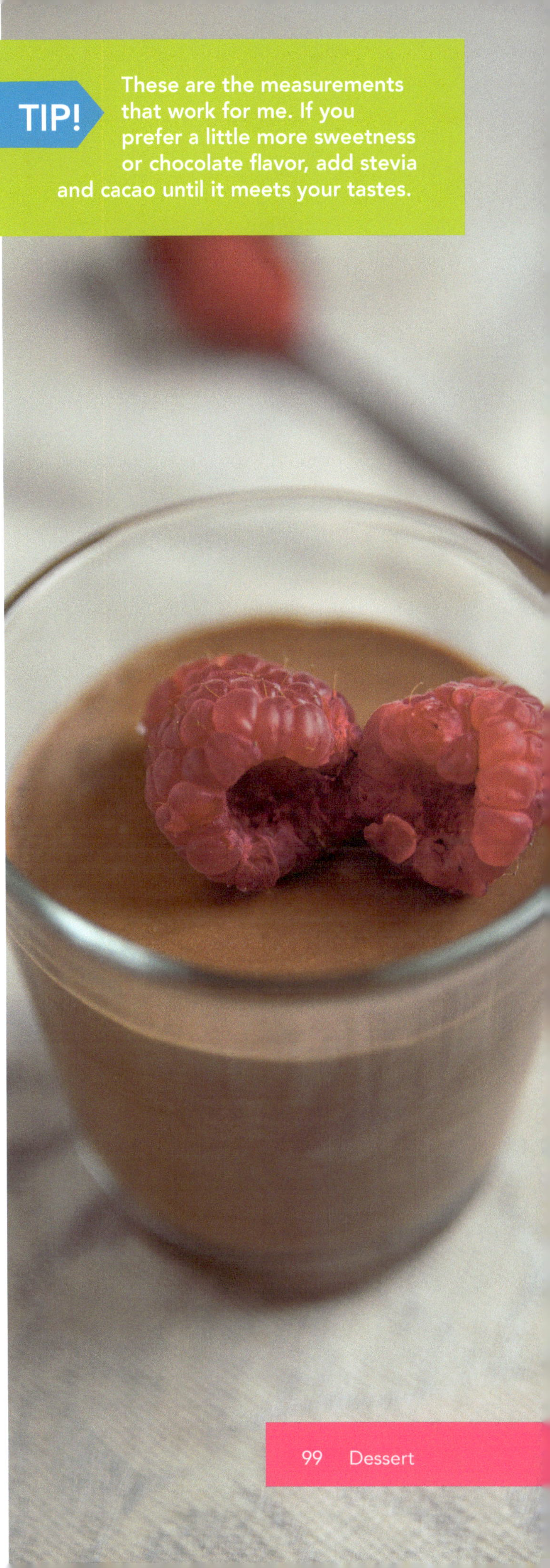

TIP! These are the measurements that work for me. If you prefer a little more sweetness or chocolate flavor, add stevia and cacao until it meets your tastes.

Honey Vanilla Chia Pudding

SERVES 3

- 1½ cups coconut milk (not canned variety)
- – seeds from ⅓ of a vanilla bean or 1 teaspoon vanilla bean paste
- 1 tbsp organic maple syrup or honey
- ¼ cup chia seeds
- – toppings like ½ cup fresh raspberries, 2 tbsp toasted unsweetened coconut flakes

COMBINE all the ingredients in a medium bowl with lid. Mix well and refrigerate.

STIR the mixture every 10 minutes for the first 30 minutes as it thickens.

COVER and refrigerate for at least 3 hours or overnight. Add more coconut milk if you would like a not-so-thick pudding

SERVE when the mixture reaches a custard-like consistency. Top with fresh fruit and coconut flakes if desired.

Dessert

Coconut Banana Pudding

SERVES 4

- 3 medium ripe bananas
- ¼ cup organic honey
- 3 tbsp cornstarch
- ⅛ tsp sea salt
- 3 large organic omega-3 egg yolks
- 1 15-ounce BPA-free can coconut milk ("lite" variety okay to use)

Optional
- ¼ cup coconut flakes, toasted

PUREÉ the bananas in food processor until smooth, then set aside.

WHISK together the honey, cornstarch, salt, egg yolks and coconut milk in a large saucepan over medium heat until smooth. Bring the mixture to a rolling boil, and then reduce the heat to a simmer. Cook, stirring constantly, until thick, about 10 minutes. To check for doneness, coat the back of a spoon with the pudding and run your finger down the center of the spoon. The pudding should hold a clear, clean line.

REMOVE from heat, and then fold in the pureéd banana.

REFRIGERATE until cool, at least two hours or up to overnight. The pudding will continue to thicken as it cools.

DIVIDE the pudding among four 4-ounce ramekins. Top each serving with toasted coconut flakes (optional). Serve cold or at room temperature.

Chocolate Stout Brownies

SERVES 16

- ⅓ cup whole wheat pastry flour
- ¼ cup unsweetened cocoa powder
- ½ tsp sea salt
- ¼ cup unsalted grass-fed butter
- 2 tbsp extra-virgin olive or avocado oil
- 4½ ounces 60-70% bittersweet chocolate, divided
- ⅔ cup coffee or chocolate stout beer
- 2 tbsp granulated sugar
- 1 tbsp brown sugar
- 1 tsp real vanilla extract
- 1 large organic omega-3 egg
- 1 large egg yolk
- – cooking spray

PREHEAT oven to 350 degrees. Lightly spoon flour into a dry measuring cup; level with a knife. Combine flour, cocoa, and salt in a medium bowl.

COMBINE butter, oil, and 3 ounces chocolate in a large bowl over simmering water. Cook over low heat until smooth, stirring occasionally. Remove from heat; cool slightly. Add beer, granulated sugar, brown sugar, vanilla, egg, and egg yolk. Beat with a mixer at medium speed 1 minute or until combined. Add flour mixture to chocolate mixture, stirring just until combined. Finely chop remaining 1½ ounces chocolate. Stir chocolate into chocolate mixture.

POUR the batter into an 8-inch square glass or metal baking pan coated with cooking spray. Bake for 30 minutes or until a wooden pick inserted in center comes out with moist crumbs clinging. Cool in pan on a wire rack. Cut into 16 bars.

NUTRITION FACTS

PER BROWNIE: 131 CALORIES, 8.5G FAT, 2G PROTEIN, 12G CARBS, 1G FIBER, 31MG CHOLESTEROL, 68MG SODIUM, 8G ADDED SUGARS

Chocolate Zucchini Bread

MAKES 1 LARGE OR 3 SMALL LOAVES

- ½ cup coconut sugar
- 2 tbsp coconut oil + more for greasing loaf pan(s)
- 2 large organic omega-3 eggs
- 1 cup unsweetened applesauce
- ¼ tsp real vanilla extract
- 2 cups whole-wheat pastry flour
- 2 tbsp unsweetened cocoa powder or cacao powder
- 1¼ tsp baking soda
- 1½ tsp ground cinnamon
- ¼ tsp sea salt
- ½ tsp instant espresso powder
- 2 cups finely shredded, unpeeled zucchini, gently pressed to remove some of the moisture
- ½ cup dark chocolate chips

PREHEAT oven to 350 degrees; lightly grease an 9x5-inch loaf pan or 3 mini loaf pans with coconut oil and set aside. In a large mixing bowl, combine the coconut sugar, 2 tbsp coconut oil, eggs, applesauce and vanilla extract. Whisk together until well-blended.

ADD the flour, cocoa powder, baking soda, cinnamon, and salt and stir to combine, taking care not to over-stir. Add the shredded zucchini and chocolate chips and fold into the mixture until well-blended.

POUR mixture into greased loaf pan and spread evenly. Place in the oven and bake for 50-65 minutes, or until a knife or toothpick comes out clean from the center of the loaf.

REMOVE Remove the pan from the oven and let rest in for 10 minutes. If desired, transfer to a wire rack to cool completely.

Pumpkin Chocolate Chip Bread

MAKES 1 LARGE OR 3 SMALL LOAVES

- 1½ cups whole wheat flour
- 1 tsp baking soda
- ¼ tsp sea salt
- – pinch of ground nutmeg
- – pinch of ground cloves
- – pinch of ground ginger
- ¾ cup canned pumpkin (not pumpkin pie filling)
- ¼ cup organic honey
- 1 tbsp extra-virgin olive or coconut oil (melted)
- 1 organic omega-3 egg
- 1 tsp real vanilla extract
- 1 tsp Stevia
- ½ cup unsweetened almond milk
- ½ cup dark chocolate chips
- – coconut oil for greasing pan(s)

PREHEAT oven to 350 degrees. Grease a 9x5-inch loaf pan or mini loaf pans with coconut oil. In a large bowl, whisk together flour, baking soda, salt, cinnamon, nutmeg, cloves and ginger.

COMBINE pumpkin, honey, oil, egg, and vanilla in a separate large bowl until well combined and smooth. Whisk in almond milk. Add wet ingredients to dry ingredients and mix until just combined. Gently fold in chocolate chips, reserving a few for sprinkling on top.

BAKE for 50 to 60 minutes or until toothpick comes out clean. Cool for 10 minutes, then remove bread from pan and transfer to wire rack to finish cooling.

NUTRITION FACTS

PER SERVING (1 LARGE SLICE OR 2 SMALL SLICES): 153 CALORIES, 4.5G FAT, 26G CARBS, 13G SUGAR, 2.3G FIBER, 3G PROTEIN

Blueberry Oat Bars

SERVES 8

- 1½ cups old fashioned oats (use gluten-free if preferred)
- ½ cup chopped raw almonds
- ½ cup dried blueberries
- ¼ cup flax seeds (sub chia seeds or hemp seeds if preferred)
- ¼ cup brown sugar
- 1 tsp sea salt
- ½ tsp ground cinnamon
- 1¼ cups milk of choice (try the *Almond Milk*, see *Other Recipes* section)
- 1 large organic omega-3 egg, whisked
- 1 tsp real vanilla extract
- – cooking spray

PREHEAT oven to 350 degrees. Stir together oats, almonds, blueberries, flax seeds, brown sugar, salt and cinnamon in a large bowl. Add milk, egg and vanilla then stir to combine.

POUR mixture into a nonstick-sprayed 8x8-inch baking dish and bake for 25 to 30 minutes, or until toothpick inserted into the center comes our clean. Cool completely then cut into bars and store in the refrigerator for 2 to 3 days, or individually wrap in saran wrap and freeze.

Zucchini Banana Bars

SERVES 8

- 1 cup whole wheat pastry flour
- 1 cup gluten-free baking flour*
- ¼ cup golden flax meal
- ⅓ cup unsweetened cacao or cocoa powder
- 2 tsp baking powder
- ¼ tsp sea salt
- ¾ cup brown or coconut sugar
- 2 large organic omega-3 eggs, lightly beaten
- ⅓ cup extra-virgin olive oil or coconut oil (melted)
- ⅓ cup unsweetened coconut or almond milk
- 1 cup finely shredded zucchini (1 medium zucchini), lightly pressed to remove some moisture
- 1 medium ripe banana, mashed
- ½ cup dark chocolate chips

If you don't have any gluten-free baking flour, use 2 cups whole wheat pastry flour.

PREHEAT oven to 350 degrees. Lightly coat a 13 x 9 x 2-inch baking dish or mini-muffin tin with nonstick cooking or baking spray; set aside. In a large bowl, combine flour, flax meal, cocoa/cacao powder, baking powder and salt. Make a small crater in center of flour mixture and set aside.

WHISK together sugar, eggs and milk in a medium bowl until well mixed. Stir in zucchini and banana. Add zucchini mixture all at once to dry ingredients. Stir just until moistened. Fold in chocolate chips. Pour batter into prepared pan or muffin tin. Bake 20 to 25 minutes or until top springs back when touched. Cool 10 minutes before removing from pan to cool completely on a rack before slicing.

NUTRITION FACTS

PER SERVING (1 BAR): 118 CALORIES, 5G TOTAL FAT, 16G CARBS, 1G FIBER, 2G PROTEIN.

Grilled Nectarines with Honey Balsamic Glaze

SERVES 6

½	cup + 2 tbsp organic honey
¼	cup balsamic vinegar
½	tsp real vanilla extract
1	8-ounce container crème fraîche
6	firm but ripe nectarines, halved, pitted

WHISK ½ cup honey, vinegar, and vanilla in small bowl. Whisk crème fraîche and remaining 2 tbsp honey in medium bowl to blend. (Glaze and crème fraîche mixture can be made 1 day ahead. Cover separately. Refrigerate crème fraîche mixture. Re-whisk both before using.)

PREPARE barbecue or grill (medium-high heat). Brush nectarines generously with half of glaze. Grill until heated through, turning occasionally, about 4 minutes. Arrange 2 nectarine halves, cut side up, on each plate. Drizzle with remaining glaze. Spoon some crème fraîche mixture into center of each nectarine half and serve.

TIP! Don't have an outdoor grill? Use a grill pan to get those grill marks on the stove over medium-high heat.

Condiments & Dressings

Practice safe lunch and dinner. Please use a condiment.

Homemade condiments and dressings always taste better than store-bought stuff. This section has some of my favorites, including a few recipes you may not have tried before like the Avocado Hummus and a Spicy Peach Salsa that is fabulous on grilled pork chops. You'll love the Smoky Barbecue Dressing over salads or as a condiment on the Herbed Turkey Burger or Veggie Burger.

Guilt-Free Guacamole

SERVES 4

- ½ pound asparagus, woody ends trimmed
- 1 ripe avocado, peeled and pitted
- 1 medium tomato, diced
- 2 garlic cloves, minced
- ¼ cup red onion, diced
- ¼ cup cilantro, minced
- – juice of ½ lime
- 1 small Serrano chili pepper, minced

STEAM the asparagus until it's bright green and tender (about 3 to 5 minutes). When cool, cut asparagus into ½-inch pieces and toss them in your blender with the other ingredients.

PULSE until the guac gets a texture you like. Season with salt and pepper.

NUTRITION FACTS

PER SERVING: 77 CALORIES, 5G FAT, 7G CARBS, 4G FIBER, 3G PROTEIN

Traditional Guacamole

SERVES 4

- 2 ripe avocados, peeled and pitted
- 1½ cups pico de gallo salsa (homemade or store-bought)
- – juice of ½ lime
- 1 garlic clove, finely minced
- ¼ tsp sea salt
- 2 tbsp fresh cilantro, minced

MASH avocados in a bowl with a fork. Add in pico de gallo and garlic and stir. Add in lime juice, cilantro and salt. Stir again and serve.

Pico de Gallo

SERVES 3

- 3 to 4 fresh plum tomatoes, diced
- ½ cup red onion, finely diced
- 1 garlic clove, finely minced
- – juice of 1 lime
- 1 tbsp jalapeño pepper, diced
- ⅛ cup fresh cilantro, chopped

STIR everything together in a medium bowl. Store in the fridge for up to about 1 week.

NUTRITION FACTS

PER SERVING (½ CUP): 30 CALORIES, 0G FAT, 6G CARBS, 19MG SODIUM

Mango Salsa

SERVES 6

- 2 large mangoes
- ½ cup red onion, finely chopped
- ½ cucumber, peeled, seeded and chopped
- ½ cup fresh cilantro, minced
- ¼ cup fresh lime juice
- 1 pinch each sea salt and pepper

PEEL mango and cut along sides of pit to remove flesh. Dice into 1-inch cubes and place into a bowl. Add remaining ingredients and mix until well blended.

NUTRITION FACTS

PER SERVING (½ CUP): 77 CALORIES, 0G FAT, 2G FIBER, 1G PROTEIN, 19G CARBS, 26MG SODIUM, 16G SUGAR

Avocado Lime Salsa

SERVES 6

- 1 large cucumber peeled, seeded and cut into chunks (about 2 cups)
- 2 avocados, peeled, pitted and cut into chunks
- ½ cup red onion, diced
- – juice of 2 limes
- – sea salt
- 2 tbsp fresh cilantro, chopped
- 2 jalapeño chili peppers, chopped + more to taste

PLACE cucumber, avocado and onion in a large bowl and add lime juice and salt. Add cilantro and chili pepper and toss gently.

Spicy Peach Salsa

SERVES 6

Most of the peaches you find in the supermarket are freestone. The flesh tears easily from the pit, making them easy to eat. If you can find white peaches, buy them; they are generally sweet and juicy and often have very little fuzz. Beware … peaches won't ripen once they're picked so look for firm, perfume-y fruit with a background color of yellow or warm cream.

- 2 large peaches with skin, pitted and diced
- 2 medium tomatoes, seeded and diced
- ¼ cup red onion, finely diced
- 2 tbsp freshly squeezed lime juice
- 2 tbsp fresh cilantro, chopped
- 1 tbsp jalapeño chili pepper with seeds, minced

COMBINE peaches, tomato, onion, lime juice, cilantro and chili pepper in a bowl.

SEASON with salt to taste and serve with tortilla chips or with grilled chicken or fish. Salsa can be made up to several hours ahead and stored in the refrigerator.

Avocado Hummus

SERVES 4 TO 6

- 1   15-ounce can cannellini beans, rinsed and drained
- 1   large or 2 small avocados, seeded, peeled and coarsely chopped
- ½   cup packed arugula
- ⅓   cup fresh flat-leaf parsley leaves
- 1   garlic clove, smashed
- 1   tsp sea salt + extra for seasoning
- ¼   tsp freshly ground black pepper + extra for seasoning
- 2   tbsp extra-virgin olive oil

COMBINE the beans, avocado, arugula, parsley, lemon juice, garlic, salt and pepper in the bowl of a food processor.

PULSE until the mixture is coarsely chopped. Gradually add the olive oil until the mixture is creamy. Season with salt and pepper.

White Bean Dip

SERVES 6

- 1   15-ounce can cannellini beans, drained and rinsed
- 2   garlic cloves
- 2   tbsp fresh lemon juice
- ⅓   cup extra-virgin olive oil + 4 tbsp
- ¼   cup (loosely packed) fresh flat-leaf parsley leaves
- –   sea salt and freshly ground black pepper
- 6   store-bought pitas
- 1   tsp dried oregano

PREHEAT oven to 400 degrees.

PLACE the beans, garlic, lemon juice, ⅓ cup olive oil and parsley in the work bowl of a food processor. Pulse until the mixture is coarsely chopped. Season with salt and pepper, to taste. Transfer the bean pureé to a small bowl.

CUT each pita in half and then into 8 wedges. Arrange the pita wedges on a large baking sheet. Pour the remaining oil over the pitas. Toss and spread out the wedges evenly. Sprinkle with the oregano, salt, and pepper. Bake for 8 to 12 minutes, or until toasted and golden in color.

SERVE the pita toasts warm or at room temp alongside the bean dip.

Condiments & Dressings   108

Simple Vinaigrette Dressing

SERVES 4

- ½ cup extra-virgin olive oil
- 3 tbsp white wine or champagne vinegar
- 1 tsp Dijon mustard
- – pinch sugar
- ⅛ tsp sea salt
- ⅛ tsp freshly ground black pepper

WHISK vinegar, mustard, salt, pepper and a pinch of sugar in a small bowl. Slowly add in oil whisking until emulsified. You can also shake the ingredients in a jar or mix in a blender.

Cilantro Lime Dressing

SERVES 4

- ¼ cup fresh lime juice (about 3 limes)
- ¼ cup white wine or rice vinegar
- 4 to 5 garlic cloves
- ½ tsp sea salt
- 2 tsp sugar
- 1 cup avocado oil
- ½ cup roughly chopped cilantro, stems removed

BLEND first five ingredients in a blender or food processor until combined. With the blender running, slowly add in oil in a steady stream. Add cilantro and blend until the cilantro has broken down but still maintains some of its texture. Use on salads and also as a marinade.

Orange Herb Dressing

SERVES 4

- 2 tbsp fresh squeezed orange juice
- 2 tbsp white balsamic vinegar or apple cider vinegar
- 2 tbsp extra-virgin olive oil
- 1 tbsp fresh tarragon, minced or ½ tsp dried tarragon
- ½ tsp fresh oregano, minced, or ¼ tsp dried oregano
- ½ tsp orange zest
- – sea salt and fresh ground black pepper to taste

PUT all ingredients into a glass jar or bowl. Shake or whisk together. Dressing will keep for several days in the fridge.

Balsamic Dressing

SERVES 8

- ½ cup extra-virgin olive oil
- ½ cup balsamic vinegar
- ¼ cup shallot, chopped
- 1 tbsp Dijon mustard
- 1 tsp Italian seasoning
- ½ sea salt
- ½ tsp freshly ground black pepper

WHISK vinegar, mustard, salt, pepper, seasoning and shallot in a small bowl. Slowly add in oil whisking until emulsified. You can also shake the ingredients in a jar or mix in a blender.

TIP! The Cilantro Lime Dressing is delicious on the *Southwestern Chop Salad* and the *Mexican Quinoa Salad*.

Smoky Barbecue Dressing

SERVES 3

- ¼ cup smoky barbecue sauce (look for a brand that's low in sugar)
- ¼ cup extra-virgin olive oil
- 2 tbsp fresh lemon juice
- 1 tbsp organic honey
- – pinch sea salt
- – tsp freshly ground black pepper

PUT all ingredients into a glass jar or bowl. Shake or whisk together. Dressing will keep for several days in the fridge.

Red Wine Vinaigrette Dressing

MAKES 1⅔ CUPS

- ½ cup red wine vinegar
- 3 tbsp fresh lemon juice
- 2 tsp organic honey
- 2 tsp sea salt
- – freshly ground black pepper
- 1 cup extra-virgin olive oil

WHISK vinegar, lemon juice, honey, salt, pepper in a small bowl. Slowly add in oil whisking until emulsified. You can also shake the ingredients in a jar or mix in a blender.

TIP! I love this dressing over romaine and leftover turkey mixture from the *Turkey Taco Lettuce Cups* recipe.

Savory Tahini Dressing

SERVES 3

- 2 tbsp tahini
- 2 tbsp freshly squeezed lemon juice
- 1 tbsp apple cider vinegar
- 1 tsp lemon zest
- – pinch sea salt and freshly ground black pepper
- 1 tsp extra-virgin olive oil

PUT all ingredients into a glass jar or bowl. Shake or whisk together. If the dressing looks too thick, add a little more vinegar. Dressing will keep for several days in the fridge.

Other Recipes

"We all eat, and it would be a sad waste of opportunity to eat badly."
— Anna Thomas

This last section has a few recipes that didn't necessarily fall into common meal categories, but it's all great stuff that while you could buy it at the store, making your own is often cheaper and tastes a whole lot better! Experiment with homemade kale chips. They're way better than store-bought and way cheaper too. The Herbed Cashew Cheese tastes great on crackers and is a good option if you are dairy free (and even if you aren't). Try making your own almond milk. Or your own granola.

Almond Milk

MAKES 2 CUPS

1	cup raw almonds
2	cups water
2	to 2½ cups filtered water

Optional
1	tsp real vanilla extract
1	pitted Medjool date

PLACE almonds in a bowl and cover with tap water. Leave to sit at least 6 hours, and preferably overnight.

DRAIN the water, and place almonds in a blender. Pour fresh, filtered water into blender, and if using sweeteners or optional flavoring agents (like dates or vanilla) add it to the blender as well. Blend until the almonds have completely broken down to a fine almost paste.

PLACE a nut milk bag inside a large bowl. Pour the liquid into the bag, pull the drawstring closed, and squeeze out liquid onto the bowl.

POUR almond milk into a glass storage jar with lid and refrigerate (I use a cone filter to help get it into the jar). The almond milk will keep fresh in the refrigerator for about 5 days. It's for this reason I don't make big batches unless I will be cooking with it.

TOSS the grounds or freeze to use later in cooking.

TIP! Homemade nut milks don't last long in the fridge, so this recipe is a smallish batch. Fresh nut milks will also separate in the fridge. That's totally normal. Just shake well before using.

Chicken Stock

MAKES 10 CUPS

12	cups filtered water
1	to 2 pounds chicken bones and gizzards (use the leftovers from your *Whole Roasted Chicken*)
1	tbsp apple cider vinegar
1	medium yellow onion, peeled and quartered
3	large carrots, cut into large dice
4	garlic cloves, smashed
2	stalks celery with leaves
2	bay leaves
1	tsp sea salt
½	tsp freshly ground black pepper
1	bunch fresh flat-leaf parsley

PLACE all of the ingredients except the parsley in a slow cooker and cook on low for 24 hours or on high for 12 hours. Turn off the slow cooker and skim the fat off the top. Stir in the parsley, cover, and let sit for 30 minutes.

STRAIN the broth through a fine-mesh sieve or cheesecloth. Store in the refrigerator or freezer for later use. Scoop off any solidified fat before using.

KEEP homemade stock in the refrigerator for up to 2 weeks or in the freezer for 6 months. Thaw overnight in the refrigerator or in a stockpot on low heat.

Honey Vanilla Granola
MAKES 3 CUPS

This may seem like a bit of work for something that can easily be store-bought. But … you get to control the ingredients and the amount of sugar that goes into your homemade granola. Plus, store-bought granola is expensive and often kinda stale!

- 3 cups gluten-free rolled oats (not instant)
- 3 tbsp packed light brown sugar
- ½ tsp ground cinnamon
- ¼ tsp sea salt
- ⅓ cup organic honey
- ¼ cup coconut oil (melted)
- 1 tsp real vanilla extract
- ½ cup small-dice dried fruit (cranberries, raisins or blueberries are a good option)
- ½ cup coarsely chopped raw or toasted nuts or seeds or both

PREHEAT oven to 300 degrees and arrange a rack in the middle. Place the oats, brown sugar, cinnamon, and salt in a large bowl and stir to combine; set aside.

ADD honey, oil, and vanilla n a small bowl and stir to combine. Pour over the oat mixture and mix until the oats are thoroughly coated.

SPREAD mixture in a thin, even layer on a rimmed baking sheet. Bake for 15 minutes, then stir and continue baking until the granola is very light golden brown, about 5 to 15 minutes more.

PLACE baking sheet on a wire rack and cool the granola to room temperature, stirring occasionally, about 20 minutes. (Note: It will harden as it cools.) Add the fruit and nuts or seeds to the baking sheet and toss to combine.

STORE granola in an airtight container for up to 2 weeks.

Parmesan Kale Chips
SERVES 3

- 1 bunch green curly kale
- ¼ cup extra-virgin olive oil
- 1 tsp sea salt
- ½ tsp freshly ground black pepper
- 2 tbsp Parmesan or Pecorino Romano cheese, freshly grated

PREHEAT oven to 350 degrees. Arrange racks so they are evenly spaced in the oven.

LAY each kale leaf on a board and, with a small sharp knife, cut out the hard stem. Tear large leaves in half. Place the kale in a large bowl of water and wash it well. Drain the kale and pat dry with paper towels. Dry bowl and put the kale back in the bowl.

TOSS the kale with the olive oil, 1 tsp kosher salt, and ½ tsp pepper. Divide the kale among 2 or 3 sheet pans and sprinkle with a light coating of cheese. Roast for 15 minutes, until crisp.

TIP! If you put too much kale on one pan, it will steam rather than roast and will never become crisp.

Herbed Cashew Cheese

MAKES ABOUT 1 CUP

1½	cups raw cashews, chopped in half if whole cashews
4	tbsp apple cider vinegar
2	tbsp freshly squeezed lemon juice
1	tsp lemon zest
3	tbsp water + water to soak the cashews
3	spring onions, diced
2	tbsp fresh chives, chopped
3	tbsp fresh flat-leaf parsley, chopped
–	pinch sea salt
–	pinch freshly ground black pepper
2	tbsp nutritional yeast

SOAK cashews in water in the fridge overnight, or up to 24 hours. In the morning drain and rinse the cashews and add to a blender or food processor with the cider vinegar, lemon juice and water, blend until smooth as possible, adding up too another 2 tbsp of water if necessary.

TRANSFER cashew purée to a mixing bowl and fold in the onions, herbs, salt, pepper and nutritional yeast. Line a small 6-inch sieve with cheese cloth and place the sieve over a bowl. Add in the cashew mixture, smooth out the top and carefully fold over the sides of the cheese cloth. Leave on the side for about two hours and discard the liquid that has drained out into the bowl.

PLACE in the fridge overnight to allow even more water to drain and the cheese to firm up. After allowing to sit overnight, carefully unfold the cheese cloth and turn the cashew cheese dome out onto a plate.

SERVE with gluten-free or regular crackers, as a dip for raw veggies, or as a spread for sandwiches and wraps.

Kale Walnut Pesto

MAKES 1 CUP

- ⅓ cup extra-virgin olive oil
- 3 cups green curly kale, chopped
- – sea salt
- ½ cup fresh Parmesan cheese, grated
- ¼ cup walnuts

TOAST walnuts in a dry sauté pan until lightly browned; let cool.

PULSE in a food processor until finely ground. Add the kale and ¼ tsp salt and pulse until finely chopped. Add the Parmesan and pulse to combine. Slowly pour in the olive oil, pulsing to incorporate.

Basil Pesto

MAKES ¾ CUP

- 2 cups fresh basil leaves
- ¼ cup pine nuts, raw or lightly toasted
- 3 garlic cloves
- ¼ tsp sea salt
- 1 tbsp fresh lemon juice
- 2 tbsp extra-virgin olive oil
- ¼ cup freshly grated Parmesan or Romano cheese

PLACE all ingredients except cheese in a blender or food processor and process until smooth.

TRANSFER mixture into a medium bowl and stir in cheese. Serve or refrigerate for up to 3 days (cover with a thin layer of olive oil to prevent browning).

Spinach Avocado Pesto

MAKES ABOUT ¾ CUP

- ½ ripe avocado, halved and pitted
- 1½ cups baby spinach
- 1 tbsp almonds or pistachios
- 1 garlic clove
- – juice of ½ lime
- – pinch of red pepper flakes
- ¼ tsp sea salt
- 1 tbsp extra-virgin olive oil

ADD flesh of the avocado, spinach, almonds, garlic, lime juice, sea salt and red pepper flakes to food processor and blend for 2 to 3 minutes, stopping to scrape down sides as needed or until smooth and creamy. If pesto is too thick, add 1 tbsp of water at a time until desired thickness. Take a taste and adjust seasoning.

ADD olive oil and blend for a few seconds to finish.

Chimichurri Sauce

MAKES ABOUT 2 CUPS

- ½ cup red wine vinegar
- 1 tsp sea salt + more to taste
- 4 garlic cloves, thinly sliced or minced
- 1 shallot, finely chopped
- 1 Fresno chili or red jalapeño, seeds removed and finely chopped
- ½ cup fresh cilantro, minced
- ¼ cup fresh flat-leaf parsley, minced
- 2 tbsp fresh oregano, finely chopped
- ¾ cup extra-virgin olive oil

COMBINE vinegar, 1 tsp salt, garlic, shallot, and chili in a medium bowl and let stand for 10 minutes. Stir in cilantro, parsley, and oregano. Using a fork, whisk in oil.

TIP! You can substitute gluten-free flour for whole wheat flour in most recipes. Just watch the consistency of whatever you're making. Sometimes when using gluten-free flours, you may need to add a little more liquid.

Other 118

Gluten-Free Flour Blend

MAKES ABOUT 5 CUPS

- 3 cups brown rice flour (preferably superfine)
- 2¼ cups sorghum flour (also called sweet white sorghum flour)
- 2 cups tapioca flour (also called tapioca starch) or coconut flour
- ¾ cup sweet rice flour (also called glutinous rice flour)
- ¾ cup potato starch (NOT potato flour)
- ¼ cup cornstarch

COMBINE all ingredients in a large mixing bowl and whisk well.

TRANSFER flour mixture to an airtight class container and store in a cool, dark place (like a pantry) if you bake often, or your refrigerator if you don't.

Trainer, Coach, Author

Jennifer Weland owns and runs Evolve Fitness & Coaching, helping clients and readers change their lives for the better through understanding their bodies and taking better care of themselves through that knowledge. She takes a realistic approach to fitness, nutrition and lifestyle behaviors because she knows it's a marathon, not a sprint. The goal is a flat belly and a strong, lean, happy body ... for life.

Jennifer trains, coaches and writes with passion, humor and the ability to inspire and motivate people to make positive lifestyle changes. In addition to working with private clients and creating online fitness programs, she is the author of this recipe guide, and the book Flat & Happy: Get a Flat Belly and Happy Body for Life. Find them on her website.

Learn more about Jennifer, and check out her fitness programs on www.evolvefitnessandcoaching.com.

Follow her on ...

 www.facebook.com/EvolveFitnessCoaching

 www.pinterest.com/EvolveFitCoach

 www.twitter.com/jweland

SECOND EDITION

www.ingramcontent.com/pod-product-compliance
Lightning Source LLC
Chambersburg PA
CBHW041544220426
43665CB00002B/35